Matthew Horace Hayes

Illustrated Horse Breaking

Matthew Horace Hayes

Illustrated Horse Breaking

ISBN/EAN: 9783743400610

Manufactured in Europe, USA, Canada, Australia, Japa

Cover: Foto ©Lupo / pixelio.de

Manufactured and distributed by brebook publishing software (www.brebook.com)

Matthew Horace Hayes

Illustrated Horse Breaking

ILLUSTRATED
HORSE BREAKING.

BY

CAPT. M. HORACE HAYES,
LATE OF 'THE BUFFS.'

AUTHOR OF "RIDING: ON THE FLAT AND ACROSS COUNTRY;"
"VETERINARY NOTES, FOR HORSE OWNERS;"
"RACING REMINISCENCES IN INDIA;"
"TRAINING AND HORSE MANAGEMENT IN INDIA," ETC.

Fifty-two Illustrations by

J. H. OSWALD BROWN.

LONDON:
W. THACKER & CO., 87, NEWGATE STREET.
CALCUTTA: THACKER, SPINK & CO.
BOMBAY: THACKER & CO. LIMITED.
1889.

LONDON:
PRINTED BY WILLIAM CLOWES AND SONS, Limited,
STAMFORD STREET AND CHARING CROSS.

CONTENTS.

Chapter	Page
I.—Theory of horse-breaking	1
II.—Principles of mouthing	41
III.—Horse-control	77
IV.—Rendering horses docile	147
V.—Giving horses good mouths.	166
VI.—Teaching horses to jump	188
VII.—Mounting horses for the first time	197
VIII.—Breaking horses for ladies' riding	209
IX.—Breaking horses to harness	212
X.—Faults of mouth	216
XI.—Nervousness and impatience of control	222
XII.—Jibbing in saddle	227
XIII.—Jumping faults	230
XIV.—Vices in harness	233
XV.—Aggressiveness	242
XVI.—Riding and driving the newly-broken horse	247
XVII.—Stable vices	251
XVIII.—Teaching the horse tricks	259
XIX.—Testing a horse's manners, mouth, and temper	271
XX.—On improvised gear	272
Appendix	274

ILLUSTRATIONS.

Fig.		Page
1.	Horse bending his neck to the rein without swinging round his hind-quarters at the same time, in answer to the pull	58
2.	Shews horse having answered the pull of off rein as he should, and consequently coming straight at his fence.	61
3.	The proper length for a standing martingale	70
4.	First loop in forming a halter	79
5.	Second step in forming a rope halter.	79
6.	Rope-halter on pole, ready for use	82
7.	Halting vicious horse with rope-halter on pole	83
8.	Pratt's method of haltering	87
9.	Noosing a fore-leg.	90
10.	Pulling up a fore-leg when noosed	91
11.	Picking up a fore-leg	95
12.	How to hold up a fore-leg	97
13.	Rarey's leg-strap	100
14.	Tying up fore-leg with stirrup leather	101
15.	The best method of fastening up a fore-leg	103
16.	A stirrup leather as used for holding up a fore-leg	106
17.	The halter-twitch.	109
18.	Do. do.	110
19.	Pratt's rope-twitch, first portion.	114
20.	Pratt's twitch completed	115
21.	Pratt's twitch on horse's head, and tightened at word "steady".	116
22.	Head-stall twitch on horse.	117
23.	The bridle-twitch, front and near-side view	119
24.	The bridle-twitch, off-side view.	120

Fig.		Page
25.—The strait-jacket		122
26.—Horse with strait-jacket on		123
27.—Picking up a hind-leg		127
28.—First step in picking up a hind-leg without the assistance of a helper		130
29.—Second step in picking up a hind-leg without the assistance of a helper		133
30.—Shewing how to fasten a rope to the end of horse's tail with a "double sheet bend"		136
31.—Hind hoof held up by two assistants with rope from tail		137
32.—Leg pulled back with one rope, a method to be avoided, as throwing the horse off his balance		139
33.—Mode of fastening a rope to a short tail		140
34.—Short-tailed horse with ropes attached to tail		141
35.—Improvised hobble made with a stirrup iron		144
36.—Wooden gag		145
37.—Crupper leading rein		149
38.—Throwing a horse by means of pulling his head round with a rope		155
39.—Horse with his head pulled round when thrown		159
40.—Best method of keeping a horse on the ground that has fallen in harness		163
41.—Horse with driving gear on		168
42.—Horse with driving pad on, new model		169
43.—Bird's-eye view of position of driver		175
44.—Driving on foot		184
45.— Do. Do.		185
46.—Horse prepared to be mounted for the first time		200
47.—Second stage in breaking a horse for riding		201
48.—Pulling kicker's head round in stall		253
49.—Tail tied with tapes to prevent horse rubbing it		257
50.—Comanche bridle, off side		262
51.—Comanche bridle, near side		263
52.—The knot on off side of Comanche bridle enlarged		264

PREFACE.

I OFFER this work to the favourable consideration of the public, as an attempt to describe a reasoned-out system of horse-breaking, which I have found, by practical experience, to be easy of execution, rapid in its effects, and requiring the possession of no exceptional strength, activity, pluck, or horsemanship by the operator, who, to become expert in it, will, as a rule, need only practice. It is in accordance with our English and Irish ideas on the subject; for it aims at teaching the horse "manners," and giving him a snaffle-bridle mouth; so that he will "go up to the bridle," and "bend" himself in thorough obedience to rein and leg.

As a personal explanation, I may mention that after having spent many years racing and training in India, during which time I practised the ordinary methods of breaking, I returned to England, where I learned the use of the standing martingale and long driving reins, as applied specially to jumpers, from Mr. John Hubert Moore, who was the cleverest "maker" of steeplechasers Ireland ever knew. He, I may remark, obtained these methods, in his youth, from an old Irish breaker, named Fallon, who was born more than a century ago. I had also valuable instruction in "horse taming" from Professor Sample. Having read an account of MM. Raabe and Lunel's "*hippo-lasso*," as a means of control for veterinary operations, I conceived, with happy results, the idea of utilising this ingenious contrivance in breaking. I also learned, about the same time, how to halter a loose horse without running any danger of being kicked, or bitten.

Having thus acquired a fair amount of information, on what has always been to me a favourite subject, I naturally wished to put it into practice.

As I knew, judging from my former ignorance, how much men in India stood in need of instruction in horse-breaking, I determined to return to that country with the object of teaching this art; so as to acquire the experience I needed, and to "pay my expenses" at the same time. I am glad to say that I was successful in both respects. During a two years' tour, I held classes at all the principal stations of the Empire—from Tricinopoly to Peshawur, and from Quetta to Mandalay—and, having met a very large number of vicious animals and fine horsemen, I obtained experience, and greatly added to my stock of knowledge, which I shall now try to utilise for the benefit of my readers. As I proceeded through India, I felt the necessity of rejecting some methods I had formerly prized, altering others, and adopting new ones; so that the course of instruction which I was able to give to my more recent classes, was far more extensive, and of better proved utility, than what I had to offer at the beginning of my travels. The great want which I had, at first, felt was a method by which a person could secure and handle, with perfect safety, any horse, no matter how vicious he might be. However, after many kicks, a few bites, and several lucky escapes, I was able to perfect the required method, which is so simple, that the only wonder is that I did not think of it before. I may explain that the Australian horses met with in India, where they form a considerable proportion of the animals used for riding and driving, are far more dangerous and difficult to handle and control, than British stock. Had I remained in England all my life, I should not have acquired a quarter of the experience of vicious horses I was afforded, during the time I lately spent in India. It goes almost without saying, that the harder the pupil is to teach, the greater chance has the instructor of becoming expert in his business. I need hardly say, that I shall, always, be very grateful to any of my readers who may favour me with special information on this, or kindred subjects.

I may mention, that, after returning from India, I held classes in England, Gibraltar, Malta, Egypt, Ceylon, Singapore, and China.

I have much pleasure in giving, in the body of this work, the sources from which I have taken various hints.

The chief claim I, here, make to originality, is, that in bringing together the results of experience in different countries, I have endeavoured to reduce the art of breaking horses to a more or less complete system, many of the principles of which, I venture to think, I have been the first to expound, and that I have made several improvements in existing methods. The new things which I have introduced need no special mention here.

My best thanks are due to Mr. J. H. Oswald Brown, for the faithful and painstaking manner in which he has illustrated the letter-press of this book. The drawings speak for themselves.

Although I am aware that the proceeding on my part may be deemed unusual; still, in order to strengthen my words, I have ventured to submit to my readers, in an appendix, the recorded opinions of various members of my classes on the practical working of the theories and methods described in this book.

I shall, at all times, be ready to give practical instruction to persons wishing to learn this art of making the horse a safe, and pleasant conveyance.

JUNIOR ARMY AND NAVY CLUB,
    ST. JAMES'S STREET, LONDON. S.W.

January 1, 1889.

ILLUSTRATED HORSE-BREAKING.

CHAPTER I.

THEORY OF HORSE-BREAKING.

Object of horse-breaking—Causes of faults which can be remedied by breaking—Vice in the horse—Distinction between nervousness and deliberate vice—Mental qualities of the horse—Association of ideas in breaking—Value and scope of breaking—On the possibility of overcoming any form of vice—Necessity for obtaining control over the horse—On the nature of the coercion to be applied to unruly horses—Punishment—Fatigue as a means of subjugation—Effect of the voice—Personal influence in breaking—Advisability of possessing various methods of breaking—A good mouth, the chief requirement—Permanency in the effects of breaking—Expedition in breaking—The ordinary method of breaking—Breaking by kindness alone—The rough and ready style of breaking—Summary of the principles of the art of rendering horses docile.

The object of horse-breaking is to teach the animal to obey the orders of his master in the best possible manner. Hence, this art includes instruction in the advantageous application of his powers, as well as methods for rendering him docile.

Causes of faults which can be remedied by breaking are :—1. Nervousness ; or the unnecessary fear of the presence or handling of man, or of the effect of any of the horse's other surroundings, which, however startling they might be to him in a wild state, he can find by experience will not hurt him.

2. Impatience of control, which frequently co-exists with nervousness, in the same animal.

3. Ignorance of the meaning of the indications used by man to convey his wishes to the horse.

4. Deliberate disobedience. There is no doubt that sulkiness of temper is, often, inherited.

5. Active hostility, which, as far as my experience goes, is, always, the result of bad treatment, whether brought on by cruelty, or by allowing a naturally fractious animal to get the upper hand.

It is evident that vices caused by disease, or infirmity, do not come within the province of the breaker.

6. The fact of having been taught some trick —for instance, kicking when touched behind the saddle—the practice of which constitutes a vice.

Vice in the Horse, from a breaking point of view, may be held to signify the practice, on the part of the animal towards man, of disobedience —wilful or otherwise—of any legitimate command; or want of docility.

The distinction between nervousness and deliberate vice may be easily made, if we observe how a horse acts after we have proved to him that he need have no fear of us. For instance, if we fix up a horse, say, in a "strait-jacket," (see page 118) so that he cannot kick, and continue to "gentle" him over with our hand, until he is thoroughly assured of the good faith of our intentions; we might justly term him a vicious brute if he kicked at us, without our touching him, the moment the restraint was removed. I may mention, in this connection, that fear of the near approach of man will often induce a purely nervous animal to kick out, if a person, and especially a stranger, ventures to come within reach. Although we may frequently find a horse kick from nervousness, he will rarely bite from that cause alone. As a verbal distinction between faults due to deliberate vice, and those caused by fear of man, or of the animal's strange surroundings, would not, generally, be understood at first glance, I need not attempt to make it in these pages.

The more experience I acquire in the breaking of horses, the more convinced I become, that the so-called "nervousness" of animals that have been handled some time, is largely made up of impatience of control, and, in many cases, of active hostility. Without, for a moment, imputing intentional deceit to a "nervous" "old stager," I make bold to assert that many crafty, dangerous brutes pose before their owners as ill-used victims of a too highly strung nervous system. Take, for instance, an aged horse, like many I have met, that snorts with apparent terror at anyone that approaches him, and is ready, on the slightest chance of reaching his mark, to strike out in front, or lash out from behind, if saddling or mounting him be attempted. His nervous emotion, the first time he was taken in hand, or the first time he began his unpleasant tricks, may have been thoroughly genuine; but its exhibition was evidently attended with the result of his more or less successfully resisting control. This act of insubordination having revealed to the horse the extent of his own power, which, to every animal, is a pleasurable sensation, was naturally repeated again and again, until the vicious habit was confirmed; although its necessity might have been, scores and scores of times, disproved by the saddling or mounting having been accomplished without the infliction of any pain to the horse, however great the trouble may have been to the groom or rider. In the case I have mentioned, the fault lay with the person who had charge of the animal, and who ought to have, then and there, mastered him the very first time he shewed resistance to a legitimate order. Whether the continued failure to resist discipline was caused by the infliction of cruelty, or by the exhibition of incompetence on the part of the man, matters little as regards their detrimental result on the animal, except, that unsuccessful punishment always aggravates a vice to a deplorable extent. I am inclined to think that really nervous horses are not as naturally "game" as their more placid fellows; while I am thoroughly convinced, that the majority of the *pseudo* nervous sort are sulky, treacherous brutes. I am, however, ready to admit that there are many exceptions to the rule I have ventured to lay down. At the same time, it would be most unwise to ignore the fact that the repetition of any trick, however it may be caused, the practice of which renders the animal difficult of control, has an increasingly bad effect on him the longer it be continued.

Mental qualities of the Horse.—The possibility of our being able to obtain an easy mastery over the horse, who is greatly our superior in strength and activity, and quite our equal in pluck, rests on the fact that instinct, rather than reason, guides his actions. To investigate this, we may try the experiment, when standing to the side and a little to the rear of a kicker, of touching him about the hocks or quarters with a conveniently long stick, when, if he "lets out" straight behind him, we may conclude that this is a purely reflex or instinctive action on his part. If the animal kicks at the stick, as the cause of annoyance, he certainly conducts himself in a manner that is not altogether irrational. But if he tries to kick the man who holds the stick, we cannot deny him the possession of reasoning power. In order that my meaning be not misunderstood, I here suppose that this experimental horse is one which would viciously kick a person who, when standing behind him, would be rash enough to touch the animal, however gently, with his hand; and not one whose kick would be more of a push—to remove an offending object—than a blow. Luckily, horses that can reason, even to such a small extent as this, are rare.

I usually teach horses to lie down (see page 153) by tying up, in the first instance, one fore-leg, arranging the necessary gear, and then making the animal forcibly "go down." Although many horses will "fight" desperately, time after time, when they are thus compelled to submit, and at a moment when they are utterly helpless, I have never found one that would resent, as a result of this hard-earned experience, the preliminary tying up of the fore-leg. But after having even once been twitched in the usual way, a horse will, as a rule, "fight" the moment his muzzle is touched. In the first case, owing to the more distant connection, the animal is unable to associate the idea of the irksome compulsion employed to make him lie down, with that of tying up his leg; apparently to us an extremely simple mental effort. In the second instance, the action of the muscles, on the hand touching the muzzle, would seem almost entirely instinctive.

The useful intelligence of the horse undoubtedly depends on the retentiveness of his memory, upon which we should work in educating him to become our faithful servant. If, however, we neglect the cultivation of this his chief mental gift, and try to gain our end by stimulating other and weaker qualities of his mind, we shall run a serious risk of spoiling his disposition. It has been often remarked to me by good judges—and it is my own experience—that teaching horses a lot of tricks, the acquisition of which demands some strain on their reasoning powers, and petting them, are very apt to cause them to become crafty and difficult to manage. In acting as I have advised, we follow the practice of judicious parents who educate their sons according to the lads' respective talents. Thus, for instance, a boy with an extremely retentive memory, but small capacity for reasoning out problems, would have a fair chance of shining as a linguist; although he would, certainly, prove a failure as a mathematician.

The feeling of self-preservation is so strongly implanted in the mind of every animal, and the retentiveness of the horse's memory is so great, that, if once the idea of his being our physical superior gets into his head, he will, naturally, be inclined to resist our commands. Hence, it is a maxim among all good breakers, that, if possible, a horse should never be allowed to know his own power. As a corollary to this, I may state that if we have a dispute as to discipline with a horse, we should not part company before making him yield; lest he may carry away the mischievous impression that he has got the best of the battle. The breaker need not attempt too much in any one lesson; but what he undertakes he should succeed in performing before quitting his pupil. For instance, with a horse that will not allow his hind legs to be touched, the breaker may reasonably content himself with making him quiet to handle about these parts, without insisting on his standing submissively to be shod behind—an operation that may be attempted on the following day. We should also make use of our knowledge of the limited scope of a horse's reasoning powers, to change the subject of contention, if we fear that there is any chance of our being worsted in a pitched battle with the animal; so that the victory —even if it does not affect the original cause of dispute—shall always remain on our side. As an illustration, I may mention the advisability of forcibly making a determined and headstrong runaway lie down, until he thoroughly "gives in"; in order to make him yield the more readily to the indications of the rein.

Association of ideas in breaking.—As association of ideas is the most valuable aid we possess to memory, we should largely utilise the practical working out of this principle in breaking. The intelligent obedience to the voice of their driver, in turning, stopping, going on, and in varying their paces, displayed by many cart-horses, is a common instance; as is, also, that of the 'bus horse, who starts onward the moment he hears the door of the conveyance slammed-to by the conductor. A friend of mine had a horse that became so increasingly difficult to mount, that at last he found it impossible to get on to him by ordinary means, on account of the animal "breaking away" the moment he attempted to put his toe into the stirrup. Living near a river, he hit on the expedient of placing the horse with his off side "broad-side on," and close to, a steep part of the bank, and then attempting to mount on the near side. As usual, when the man's foot touched the iron, the horse swung round, and, on this occasion only, fell down twenty feet into the river. The effect of this lesson, which was entirely harmless, was to make the animal perfectly steady to mount, so long as he stood on the bank of the river, in a position similar to that from which he had had his tumble; but he was just as difficult to mount as ever, anywhere else. Such a method, to be perfect, should be of universal, and not of local, application. I may add, with reference to my remarks on page 4, that my friend's unruly brute of a horse would, by many, be deemed a nervous creature, and a worthy recipient of any amount of kindness and petting. The most effective means of applying the principle of association of ideas to the breaking of vicious horses, is one by which the animal arrives at the right conclusion from wrong premisses; as with Pratt's rope-twitch (see page 113), when making a horse steady to mount. Evidently mistaking the cause of the pain inflicted on him by its employment, he connects the idea of punishment with the word "steady," and not with the application of the cord. Were he able to argue rightly on this subject, he would remain quiet only when the twitch was on, and would entirely disregard the verbal admonition, for which he entertains such marked respect.

Value and scope of breaking.—The scope of breaking is wider than persons might generally imagine; for not alone does it include the education of the untutored animal, but it also embraces the correction of faults, which, while seriously detracting from the horse's value, are usually looked upon as unavoidable dispensations that

VALUE OF BREAKING.

have to be borne with becoming philosophy; as, for instance, prancing and refusal to walk quietly, when "fresh"; chucking up the head; stargazing; boring to one side; shewing excitement in harness when the whip is cracked; shying off the ball at polo; refusal to stand perfectly steady when being mounted; etc. I need hardly say that the knowledge, which I shall endeavour to impart to my readers, of the art of giving a horse a snaffle-bridle mouth and to render him steady and reliable, is of infinitely more value to everyone, except, perhaps, to the showman who requires an advertisement, than instruction, which I shall also supply, in methods for taming man-eaters, and other exceptionally dangerous animals. This art of "horse taming" is of very little practical use; for the need of its application is of but rare occurrence. Even the celebrated Rarey, after subduing three or four "savages," when in England, had to content himself with exhibiting them about the country, as reformed characters, for lack of new subjects on which to shew his skill. When wishing to form a class for practical instruction in breaking, during my tours, I have frequently met with the objection that there were no vicious horses in that particular place. As I always replied that I needed animals with only common faults of mouth and temper, I was never at a loss for subjects to demonstrate the fact, that there are but few horses that are entirely free from some riding or driving fault, which, more or less, impairs their value, and which, as a rule, can be readily overcome. The more frequent vices I have encountered among army horses are: unsteadiness at mounting; "rushing" at fences; refusing to quit the ranks; refusing to jump; buckjumping (among Australian horses); and "difficult to shoe behind."

On the possibility of overcoming any form of vice.—The influences which man, being the weaker animal, can apply to making the horse obedient to his wishes, are: affection; the natural submission yielded by an inferior to a superior intellect; fear; and the impression—which is, generally, erroneous—that the order given cannot be resisted. The first three are the usual means for rendering docile a high-couraged horse. Although we may, to a certain extent, use the last-mentioned influence with quiet horses, and, especially in mouthing, we should remember that it is our last resource, when all others fail, in reducing a rebellious animal to submission. If, however, the horse which we have taken in hand, happen to reason sufficiently well to enable him to "see through" our artifices, our labour will, of course, be in vain. Herein lies the whole question of success, or failure, in making vicious horses docile. Man-eaters, like the historic Cruiser, the taming of whom made Rarey famous, being actuated, almost entirely, by instinctive hostility, yield far more readily to authority, than the sulky animal that, having found out a method by which he can thwart the wishes of his would-be master, craftily adheres to it, with a fair show of reason on his side. I may mention that the assertion made by many "horse-tamers," that they can cure any horse of any kind of vice, is manifestly absurd.

Of all forms of vice, those caused by stubbornness are the most difficult to eradicate; for the animal which sets its will in deliberate opposition to ours, fights us with the weapons— those of reason—by which, alone, we are, usually, superior to it. A horse that objects, from nervousness, or from mere impatience of control, to have its hind quarters handled, will quickly submit; as will, also, in the vast majority of cases, a "refuser," or jibber in saddle; if they be broken in the manner which will be explained further on. A jibber in draught, however, is apt to find out, that although the breaker is all-powerful, when it has no harness on; the advantage is all the other way, as soon as it gets between the shafts; it being easier, as Professor Sample used to say, to break a horse than to break a horse *and* trap. Besides this, it is impossible, in many cases, to directly apply breaking methods to animals in harness, in the same manner as we can do in saddle. For instance, if a trapper be accustomed to jib, as soon as it comes to a stiff incline; to back into the ditch, or fence; and, then, to proceed to kick the vehicle to pieces; all that the breaker can do, is to take it out, and endeavour to, indirectly, counteract the fault in some convenient place. He may succeed, to all appearance; although the pupil may forget the instruction received, if anything goes wrong, such as an abrupt halt, which cannot always be avoided, the first time the horse is driven up a hill in a crowded thoroughfare. In such a case, if the animal "shows fight," it will, almost to a certainty, gain the victory, and the good influence of the previous teaching will be lost. For vices unconnected with harness, on the contrary, the breaker can always find some suitable spot on which to work his will on the disobedient one, under every advantageous condition. I say this with every reasonable reserve; for we may meet with cases, sometimes, of saddle vices—such as running away on a race-course, only, when galloped—to which it is difficult to directly apply efficient breaking methods.

Unless when caused by disease, as, for instance, chronic sexual excitement in the mare, defects of vision, and pain in the legs or feet, which might make a horse refuse to jump, practically speaking, almost any riding or driving vice (I naturally exclude those vices that concern the veterinary surgeon, and not the breaker) can be overcome in time, say within a week or ten days; although I readily admit that I have been beaten in a few cases (about two per cent. of faulty horses) when my time was limited, or when I did not possess the experience I have since acquired.

I have had many hundreds of horses with various forms of "pain in the temper" pass through my hands, and, out of all these, selected from thousands of other animals, I met with only one or two which I would call incapable of being made serviceable on account of absolute idiocy. Hence, I conclude that cases of marked mental aberration are extremely rare in the horse. I do not think that I met with more than one horse which appeared incapable, from natural nervousness, of being rendered quite steady.

As the breaker has to work on the material at hand, and as he has no power to change the nervous organisation of the animal, however well he may establish the habit of implicit obedience, it is impossible for him to make a naturally sulky animal work with the gaiety of heart and pluck, that an honest horse will display.

Necessity for obtaining control over the Horse.—

In order to fulfil the necessary conditions of safety for himself, the breaker should be able, by the system under which he works—to quote the words of that admirable horse-master, Professor Sample—to make the animal rideable and driveable before he is either ridden or driven. The breaker who employs the ordinary methods, is not alone exposed to danger when mounting, or even driving his pupils' for the first few times; but also in the preliminary handling, unless, indeed, in the case of young foals. The advice to go boldly up to the horse and show him that you are not afraid of him, so freely tendered on such occasions, should be treated by its recipient as a piece of "cheap swagger," or the outcome of pretentious ignorance; for, even granted that such a demeanour would efficiently soothe a terrified animal, or cow a treacherously-disposed one—suppositions that are altogether absurd—such counsel would in no way supply the necessary foolhardiness for such an undertaking. My advice to either amateur or professional is, never to give a horse a chance of doing wrong; so, in order to be consistent after having said this, I shall endeavour to describe a method by which any horse, unsecured, say, in a yard or loose box, can be brought under complete control with, practically speaking, no risk to the operator.

On the nature of the coercion to be applied to unruly Horses.—The only risk run in enforcing the obedience which it is absolutely necessary to exact from unruly horses, is that of spoiling the animal's pluck and spirit—a contingency that can be incurred only when the fractiousness arises from "nervousness," or from want of comprehension; for what we term pluck and spirit in the horse should have no taint of stubbornness. The coercion employed should, naturally, be limited to what would be sufficient to overcome the wilfulness; for we should never employ a general effect, when a particular one will answer our purpose. Thus, suppose we had a high-couraged, generous animal, that had been made difficult to mount by a bad rider, on various occasions, prodding the horse in the side with his toe, when attempting to get into the saddle, we might get control over the animal by Pratt's twitch (see page 113), or by tying him head and tail, and then prove to him that we would not touch him with our toe, when mounting. The Rareyfying of such an animal for this or any similar fault, would be injudicious in the extreme; as it would, almost to a certainty, injuriously affect one of his most valuable qualities, namely, his pluck. As a sulky animal has little or no pluck to lose ; we may well content ourselves in gaining his obedience without troubling ourselves much about any possible deterioration of his courage.

Punishment.—The chief practical reasons against the employment of punishment in the breaking of horses are : that it is very liable to fail in its object ;

and that it is calculated to break the spirit of high-couraged animals, and to increase the sulkiness of stubborn ones. Of course I don't mean to say that a vigorous "shaking up," and a sharp cut or two with a stick (for preference), or whip, is not advisable for stopping the exhibition of "calfish" tricks by a young colt. Owing to the galling failures I have had—they were not many, for I stopped in time—I have made it a rule for my own guidance, never to touch a mare, so as to hurt her, when breaking.

I am aware that punishment, pushed to extreme limits, has, often, proved efficacious in reducing an animal to obedience, when all other means have failed. As it would, then, amount to gross cruelty, I cannot recommend its adoption in this form.

Fatigue as a means of subjugation.—Fatigue may be used as a valuable adjunct to other means of breaking, but should seldom be employed alone;

its effect, usually, appearing to be as transitory as the sensation itself. Thus, if we, while riding or driving a bolter, in order to cure him of his vice, allow him to run himself to a stand-still, we shall, in all probability, find the animal quite as ready, if not more so, to run away, the next time he is "fresh." In such a case, the fact of the horse having been allowed to do the very thing he wanted to accomplish, in defiance of the wishes of his would-be master, can have no possible effect in forming in him the habit of obedience. Fatigue may, often, appear to be the sole cause of the quietness evinced by an animal under treatment of some of the breaking methods I describe. This, however, will, on investigation, be found to be incorrect. Even the fatigue caused in, say, rendering an unruly horse quiet to shoe behind, by keeping him on the ground and "gentling" him (see page 157), is out of all proportion small compared to the amount of control obtained. One of the best examples I know of the fact, that it is the feeling of powerlessness to rebel, and not the sensation of fatigue, that compels obedience by these methods, is furnished by the experiment of making a violent horse, like an Australian buckjumper, quiet to mount in the manner described on page 197 ; the effect produced being striking ; the feeling of helplessness, evident ; and the amount of fatigue, small.

Effect of the voice.—The human voice has a powerful controlling effect over the horse. To apply it to advantage, the same tone and the same word or words should be invariably used to express the same meaning. All ambiguity of sound should be avoided. The words employed should be expressed in a decided manner, and in a clear tone of voice. I have seen some very dangerous animals approached and handled by "shouting at" them, and adopting a resolute manner, when going up to them in the stable. A horse, undoubtedly, recognises the voice more quickly than the appearance of a man.

Personal influence in breaking.—For obtaining quick results, the breaker should have the horse entirely to himself; so that no disturbing influence may distract the animal's attention. The great objection to the practice of personal influence, as a breaking agent, is that, although the animal may be perfectly obedient to the man who has had the exclusive handling of him, he may be refractory with other people, and may, even, jealously resent any interference from an outsider. I have frequently been struck with this fact when breaking savage horses who would, if they could help it, allow no one, except their groom, to meddle with them; for I always found that they were far more vicious to approach when their stable attendant was holding them, than when he was absent. We may often see the same trait of character evinced by dogs that would fly at any stranger who dared to touch them, as long as they were with their master; although they might be fairly amiable if he were not present. However much we may admire, in the abstract, this fidelity to one, in the horse, it is very apt to detract from the animal's usefulness under civilised conditions, especially, if the owner be not regarded as the confidential friend in question. When the groom is the object of this exclusive form of affection, it is generally advisable to have him changed for a new man. If a horse has to be rendered serviceable for general, as well as particular use, the breaker should refrain from accomplishing his ends by the exercise of his own personal influence, and hence, should get him to obey by rein and leg, rather than by voice and petting.

Advisability of possessing various methods of breaking.—As the removal of the cause is the only proper plan for the treatment of either disease, or vice, and as these causes differ, the breaker, to be successful, should be provided with various methods for enforcing his commands. Hence, we may rest assured that the horse-tamer who advertises his one particular method, as a certain cure for all forms of vice, is as arrant a quack as the man who foists on the public a pill for the removal of every kind of disease. In the following pages I shall describe various breaking methods, which the reader can apply according as he recognises the cause of resistance to his wishes, or of inability to understand them.

Giving a Horse a good mouth, the chief requirement in breaking.—The horse's mouth ought to be the foundation of all good breaking; for an animal with a good mouth can hardly "do wrong"; unless, indeed, under very exceptional circumstances. As it is impracticable to be constantly repeating any "taming" method, such as Rareyfying, or tying a horse by his head and tail, we must disregard such practices as means for the maintenance of a permanent state of discipline—however useful they may be for enforcing authority in the first instance—and must trust to the influence of the rein, which is ever constant on the mouth, when riding or driving, to keep the horse mindful of his duty when in action. The use of the leg should, of course, not be neglected in riding. The taming methods will, naturally, be required with animals that are difficult to handle when dismounted, or when out of the shafts.

Permanency in the effects of breaking.—The primary step to establish the habit of obedience, is, naturally, to make the horse obey in the first instance, and then to repeat the process as may be needed. Such a procedure is thoroughly rational; for it is founded on the fact that force of habit is the strongest influence which rules the equine mind. I have often, what I think unjustly, incurred blame because, after I had practically demonstrated to my pupils the feasibility of making a confirmed jibber, obstinate refuser, or almost unrideable buckjumper, willing and quiet in one lesson, that such animals have, in the course of time, become just as bad as ever; on account of their respective owners not taking the trouble, as advised by me, of repeating the easy methods I shewed. The reason men usually fail to subdue "difficult" horses, is because they do not know how to take the first step towards making the animal obedient. If, however, they be supplied with this all-important information, their task should be one of increasing facility after each repetition; and, if persevered in, would be rapidly completed; but it must be repeated until the desired habit is established.

However well a horse may have been broken of a bad habit, he will be far more likely to acquire it again under bad management, than he would have been, had he been originally free from it; for no course of discipline, although it may keep the animal under thorough control, can efface out of his mind the memory of the practice of a former habit. I need scarcely say that injudicious treatment will always be capable of spoiling any horse, whether invariably quiet, or reformed. Hence, a teacher of breaking will be wise to confine himself to showing "how it is done," and not to risk his reputation in making the impossible attempt of *permanently* "curing" a vicious horse. Besides, it is only "human nature" for the owner of an animal that has reverted to his evil courses, to blame the breaker, and not himself.

Expedition in breaking.—In order to give some idea of the possibilities of the system of breaking which I advocate and practise, I may state that, by it, any unhandled horse, no matter how wild or how old he may be, can be made quiet to ride and obedient to the ordinary indications of the rein, in from, say, two to four hours. Such a horse, to become a reliable "conveyance," would, probably, require about six more lessons—two a day—of an hour and a half's duration each. He ought, by that time, to have acquired a good mouth, steady paces, and "cleverness" to jump any ordinary fence. Army remounts that have never had even a halter on them, should, on an emergency, speaking generally, be fit for the riding-school in a couple of days. I need not dwell on the value of such expedition in military exigencies, and in all cases where time is an object. "Spoiled" horses, such as jibbers, rearers, kickers, and buckjumpers, that have learned to know their own power, would, naturally, take longer to break, than entirely unhandled animals; although the limit of five days need not, usually, be exceeded even with them. The possibility of horses going back to their old tricks may always be provided against by judicious repetition of the necessary discipline, which will be very rarely needed after the first three or four days, if the animal be "mouthed" in the manner. I shall hereafter describe. Without using any forcible methods, which, as a rule, would not be required with a valuable horse, the breaker ought not to need more than a week to make any ordinary horse thoroughly fit for all the usual requirements of saddle or harness.

To those who might advance the argument that because the ordinary method of breaking takes

ORDINARY BREAKING. 35

about ten times as long as the system I advocate, it must, therefore, be more permanent in its influence, I would beg to submit that such a contention would hold good, only, on the untenable supposition that the effects of the respective processes were equal in force. I see no possible benefit, except the very questionable one of giving the animal an exaggerated opinion of his own powers of resistance, in taking a month to accomplish what may be quite as efficiently done in an hour; as, for instance, making a fractious horse steady to mount, or quiet to shoe behind, or a sulky refuser to jump kindly. We must surely admit that the repetition of an effect, and not the time occupied in its production, is the cause of the permanency of its influence.

The ordinary method of breaking.—The usual method of rendering horses docile by early and continued handling, followed by patient and skilful riding, answers fairly well with men who regard breaking as a pleasure, and have plenty of spare time to indulge their taste in this respect. It is, however, inapplicable to circumstances under which the number of animals to be broken is out of proportion to the supply of labour; especially in the case of inexpensive stock. It is, also, besides being tedious, often ineffective in the reduction to obedience of "spoiled horses," and of those that have been allowed to run wild for a considerable time before being "taken up"; the reason being, that it does not supply us with means for enforcing our commands, then and there, on exceptionally unruly animals, which, in order to be rendered docile, must be confirmed in the habit of obedience.

Breaking by kindness alone.—While fully admiring the kindness of heart of those enthusiasts who regard a horse as a friend to be won by affection, I must say that the better plan for making him a useful member of society, is to treat him as a servant who has to be taught his work, and from whom implicit obedience has to be demanded. Until he does his work honestly and well, the less petting he gets the better; for he is an animal that is very apt to become headstrong and fractious, by a small amount of indulgence in his own way. I entirely deprecate any fighting with the horse, or punishment with whip and spur, which he can resist; but I insist on the necessity—after proving to the horse that he has nothing to fear, and after teaching him to understand one's wishes—of shewing that he must obey. I shall endeavour, in due course, to explain to the reader how such obedience can be peremptorily enforced.

The rough and ready style of breaking.—The method of reducing a horse to discipline, by forcibly securing him, getting on his back, and sticking on until he bucks himself to a standstill, is applicable only to unbroken animals of a more or less mature age, whose owners demand nothing further, than to have them made " quiet to ride." The objections to this method, as far as I can see, are: that it is not always possible to obtain the services of a rider of sufficient pluck and adhesiveness; that some horses, by "throwing themselves over," can get rid of any man off their back; that if the horse wins the fight, the victory will have the effect of making him much worse than he was before; that the mastery, even if the process be repeated, is, often, not permanent, especially with a new rider; that it is apt to spoil the horse's mouth; and that, in the case of nervous or sulky animals, it is liable to increase their particular faults. The buckjumping style of breaking is, of course, only good as far as it goes, and has no just claim to teach the manners that make the horse, as assuredly as they do the man.

Summary of the principles of the art of rendering Horses docile may be summed up as follows :

1. To obtain control over the animal.

2. To prove to him that he has nothing to fear from us, or from the surroundings in which we place

him: in other words, to give him "confidence" and cure him of "nervousness."

3. To teach him to understand the meaning of the indications by which we desire to convey our orders to him.

4. To make him obey our orders in the most implicit manner, in the event of his offering deliberate resistance to them.

5. To instruct him how to use his powers to the best advantage.

6. To make, by repetition, these acts of obedience and "cleverness" thus taught, into confirmed habits; so that the horse, who is, essentially, an animal of habit, may become a permanently useful servant.

As an illustration, I may say that we should conduct the education of a colt or filly, according to the principles we should adopt with a recently-caught young savage whom we desired to make a useful servant. While shewing him that we had complete control over him, we should prove to him that he had nothing to fear from us, and, in doing so, would gain his confidence and affection. We should teach him our language, and, according as he understood our words, so should we demand implicit obedience to our orders, and would, thus, quickly establish the desired habit.

CHAPTER II.

PRINCIPLES OF MOUTHING.

Making a horse obey the rein—Manner in which a horse should carry his head and neck, when in motion—Suitability of the horse to the bridle—How the mouth-piece should act—Teaching the horse to bend his neck to the rein—Proper direction for the pull of the reins—The running martingale—Bearing reins, side reins, and running reins—Teaching the horse to turn—Reining back—Lunging—Good hands—Snaffles and curbs—Elastic reins on dumb jockeys—The standing martingale—Nose-bands.

Making a Horse obey the rein.—In mouthing, we should act on the principle I have advocated, in the preceding chapter, of making our equine servant accord ready obedience to the lawful commands of his master; after we have taught him to understand our wishes expressed by the proper "indications." The breaker will do well always to bear in mind the old maxim, that "a horse should never get the chance of pulling successfully against the bit, or unsuccessfully against the collar." As a man on foot has as thorough command over a horse, as the animal has over its rider—supposing that both know how to exercise their respective powers—the breaker should, naturally, commence his mouthing lessons on foot, and should, as a rule, refrain from giving the horse the advantage of having him in the saddle, until the habit of obedience to rein, leg, and, if need be, to voice, is fully confirmed. In all this, we act on the retentiveness of the horse's memory, which is his strongest mental quality, in guarding ourselves from the ill consequences that might ensue from the exercise of the animal's reasoning powers, which, luckily for us, are comparatively feeble, or from his natural impatience of control.

With some horses, especially with those that have learned to know their own power, the process of inculcating the habit of obedience to the rein, by simply working on the horse's mouth, may be ineffective, or may be too tedious for practical requirements. In such a case, I would advocate the advisability of exacting obedience, in the first instance, by some readily feasible method, as advocated on page 11; so as to impress the animal with the idea of our supreme power over him, and to banish from his mind any thought of resisting our will, even on a point concerning which he would always prove victorious, had he sufficient intelligence to see through our artifice. Our power over the horse, when we are on his back, being necessarily limited in extent, it follows that, with all our teaching, we may, at times, be unable to control our mounts.

Although young horses, well bred and truly shaped, will, generally, "carry" themselves to the best advantage, we may find that many animals, even in a state of freedom, and, more particularly, those that have been in bad hands, contract a stiff and awkward carriage, which, as a rule, may be easily remedied by two or three days' "mouthing," on the system I shall describe further on, followed by good handling and the ordinary routine of saddle, or harness work. I in no way mean to say that careful riding or driving would not, *in time*, accomplish the object in view, without the aid of the work on foot; but I maintain that the preliminary mouthing is invaluable in the saving of time, and that it can produce effects which are unattainable by any rider, however good his hands may be.

Manner in which a Horse should carry his head and neck, when in motion.—When the animal takes a stride to the front, the fore-limb, which is connected to the body by muscular attachment, is drawn forwards and upwards by certain muscles of the neck; their action being naturally regulated by the depression or elevation of the head. If the head be unduly raised, the forward reach of the fore-legs will be curtailed by this "high" style of going; and the speed will, consequently, suffer.

If, on the contrary, the head be brought down too low, the animal, if at the gallop or canter, instead of "going level," will have a more or less pitching motion, from too much weight being thrown on his forehand; and will lose time in his stride by excessive bending of his knees, which is necessary to enable his feet, in that case, to clear the ground.

Owing to the variety in the conformation of different horses, and in the work they are called upon to do, it is impossible to lay down any fixed rule as to the angle at which the neck should be carried: a fact that is of little moment; as experience will enable us to form a sufficiently near approximation for all practical purposes.

The neck muscles, which draw the fore-limb forward, will naturally act to the best advantage when the neck vertebræ are extended on each other; that is, when the neck is straight. According as the neck is bent, so will this forward "pull" be diminished.

The chief muscle that draws the fore-limb

forward is attached to the head in such a manner, that it acts best when the head is carried, more or less, at right angles to the neck. Hence, we may take for granted, especially, as the correctness of the assumption can be verified by experience, that this position of the head is the best one for requirements demanding the exhibition of speed, or strength. For military purposes, "pace" is to some extent sacrificed for obtaining increased control and "handiness."

Suitability of the Horse to the bridle.—When the horse carries his head and neck in an easy, natural manner, in fact, in the best one for the display of his powers—as we have seen in the preceding paragraphs of this chapter—the mouthpiece of the snaffle will rest on the "bars" of the mouth, as long as the reins are held not much above the level of the withers. Hence, from the peculiar conformation of the horse, we obtain two special advantages for rendering him obedient to the rein. First, the "bars"—that portion of the gums of the lower jaw which are devoid of teeth and which are in front of the molars—are singularly suitable for the application of pressure; being sensitive and smooth. Secondly, when the horse carries his head and neck in the best manner for facilitating his movements, the mouth-piece will be in the position easiest for the rider or driver to control the animal by the reins. The breaker's task, therefore, as regards the carriage of the horse's head and neck, will simply be to teach him to carry them in a perfectly natural way.

How the mouth-piece should act.—If an impetuous, hard-pulling horse gets his head up and tries to "break away" with a good rider, the man will ease the reins, "drop his hands," and wait till the animal lowers its head, before he takes a pull: a rule that is followed by all our best horsemen. When the animal finds its head released, he will quickly bring it "down." The reasons for not pulling at the reins when the head is "up," are: that, when it is carried in this position, the mouth-piece falls on the corners of the mouth, pressure against which, we find by experience, is not effective in restraining the horse; and that the horse will not, as a rule, lower his head as long as the rider continues to haul on the reins. As soon as the head is brought down into its natural position, the pressure of the mouth-piece will fall on the bars. We may readily conceive, that far more pain results from the superficial nerves of the bars being squeezed between two hard bodies—the mouth-piece and the bone—than that caused by pressure on the loose and mobile tissue which forms the corners of the mouth. If, in the case I have imagined, the horse tries to get his head too low down, our typical good rider will endeavour to make the animal bring it into its proper position. The relief to the mouth obtained by arching the neck and bringing the chin close in to the chest, as some hard-mouthed horses will do, is due to a portion of the pull of the reins being, then, taken by the crown-piece of the bridle; instead of the whole of the pressure, as it should do, falling on the bars. A horse may, also, by stretching his head out, get the mouth-piece off the bars, and on to the corners of the mouth. It is needless to say that such actions on his part, are done with the object of "saving" the mouth. As they are opposed to the possession of proper control over the horse, the breaker should teach him to abandon, if he has learnt, these tricks, and to acquire the habit of bending his neck to the rein, and slackening his speed, as his sole defence against the pressure of the mouth-piece. The only alternative I can see for the use of pressure on the bars, would be its application on the nose by some form of nose-band.

Teaching the Horse to bend his neck to the rein.— Having taught the horse to hold his head, when he is ridden or driven, in an easy, natural position—

E

namely, in one that will allow the mouth-piece always to rest on the bars—we must then teach him, on the reins being "felt," to bend his neck in order to "save" his mouth. The partial check to the action of the muscles that draw the fore-limb forward, caused by the bending of the neck (see page 45) will be an easily understood signal to the animal to moderate his pace.

Proper direction for the pull of the reins.—When the horse is in motion, the forward propulsion by the hind-legs is given through the hip-joints; while that by the fore-limbs, passes through, we may roughly say, the elbow-joints. As the former impetus greatly exceeds the latter, we may assume that the centre of motion is a little in front of, and a little below the level of, the hip-joints. To comply with mechanical requirements, any pressure of the bridle on the mouth must, therefore, be in the direction of this centre of motion, so that the regularity of the stride may be interfered with as little as possible.

The rule, taught by experience, of holding the hands, when riding, and especially when galloping, just below the withers, is in entire agreement with this fact.

If the rider's hands be unduly raised, so as to make the horse carry his head too high, there will be too much weight put on the hind-quarters.

As a point of interest, I may state that, under ordinary circumstances, when a horse begins to tire in his gallop, he will, instead of "going level," throw increased weight on his forehand, and his croup, when his hind-quarters make their stroke, will become more and more raised. To accurately express this "dwelling on his stride," we may say, that as the horse becomes fatigued, the forward motion becomes, proportionately, converted into one of rotation, the chief cause of this being that the weight of the rider falls principally on the forehand. Hence, we find that, at the finish of a race, a good jockey "sits down" in his saddle, "catches a good hold" of the animal's head, and holds his hands a little above the withers: actions on his part which tend to relieve the horse's forehand of weight, and, consequently, to make him use his powers to the best advantage.

In military riding, which demands special control over the animal's movements, the horse's head is drawn in, and the rider's hand raised, much more than they would be in ordinary work.

The running martingale.—The legitimate uses of this gear are to aid in keeping the horse straight, and to prevent the reins going over his head; but not to keep the head down. If this martingale be so short as to exert a downward pull on the reins, too much weight will be thrown on the forehand. If the horse raises his head even when this martingale is lengthened out, so as to bring its rings on a level with the withers, when it is pulled up, the downward direction of the reins, from the mouthpiece to the rings of the martingale, will produce the same ill effect. Hence, it is a maxim among all good jockeys, that the head of the race-horse, with whom a level style of galloping is one of the chief essentials to success, should be kept down by the rider's hands, and not by the running martingale. It is the custom, therefore, among jockeys, when they use this gear, to lengthen it out, so that, when it is drawn up, to test its length, its rings will come up to the angle of the lower jaw, when the head is held in a natural position—a length which will obviate any chance of there being a downward pull on the reins.

In the training of a race-horse that "star-gazes," the use of a running martingale, in order to keep his head down, besides interfering with his action, is detrimental to the soundness of his legs and feet, by reason of the extra weight thrown, thereby, on his forehand.

Respecting the injurious effects of hampering the action of the neck muscles, and of putting a severe downward pressure on the mouth, especially during rapid motion, I may quote the following interesting extract from 'White's Veterinary Art,' which was written many years ago : " There is a great danger, however, of attempting to make the mouth at the time of riding, by means of a running rein ; for if he is a stubborn or runaway horse, there is great danger of throwing him down, and in the most dangerous manner that can be. For, if he is determined to run away, and the rider endeavours to prevent him by a running rein, in drawing the nose down to his chest, the muscles of the shoulder are so restrained that he must of necessity pull him down topsy-turvy. Since the body being propelled by the muscles of the hind parts, the restraint thus imposed upon the extensor muscles of the fore-leg, prevents their being thrown out to the extent required, and he comes down with the most dangerous violence. I have known this accident happen with horses that have had upright shoulders and very well-formed hind parts ; and I have also known very safe horses, that have contracted a habit of going with their noses poked out, become very unsafe, and soon get broken knees by the endeavour to improve their carriage by a martingale or running rein."

Bearing reins, side reins, and running reins.—I would dispense with the use, in breaking, of these three appliances, as ordinarily employed; for the first acts by exerting pressure on the corners of the bars, while the other two tend to keep the head in an unnaturally low position. Were the side reins lengthened out so as to act as a properly arranged standing martingale (see **page** 70), or were the running reins attached high up on the saddle; as near as possible on the level of the withers, their use would be wholly unobjectionable. With the long reins (see page 172), the standing martingale (see page 70), and driving pad (see page 166), the horse can be quickly taught to carry himself properly, without any injurious effect being produced.

Teaching the Horse to turn.—When we fail to make a horse turn properly, we find, almost always, that our want of success is due to the animal's hind-quarters not "coming round" in concert with his head and neck, which, as a rule, can be "bent" to the right or left with facility. I venture to dissent, with all diffidence, from the principle of the "suppling" lessons enjoined by that great master of equitation, M. Baucher, as first steps for "forming the mouth," for teaching the horse to bring his head round to one side or the other, according to the indication used, while the hind limbs remain fixed. To my thinking, precision in the simple movements of advancing to the front, reining back, and turning, should be sought for, before attempting any artificial evolutions,—such as the "passage," and "shoulder-in,"—only, in which, the bending of the head and neck is made independently of that of the hind-quarters. As, in riding, all turns should be made with the aid of the support of the "outward leg"—a fact too widely recognized for the

Fig. 1.—Horse bending his neck to the rein without swinging round his hindquarters at the same time, in answer to the pull.

necessity of proof here—we should teach our pupil, from the outset, to avail himself of such assistance. As the rider's weight tends to advance the position of the centre of gravity, the natural turn, especially at fast-paces, will be a compromise between the turn "on the centre," and that " on the haunches." I may remark, that the further the weight is thrown back, and the greater is the support of the outward leg, the more will the turn be made on the haunches. The use of this leg-pressure, although necessitated by the unequal distribution of the rider's weight, is, besides this, valuable in all sharp turns made at speed. The turn "on the forehand" can be taught by the rider, after the simpler one is mastered. In treating about turning, I draw no distinction between the saddle and harness horse; for the latter should be made as "clever" as the former, in "collecting" himself and "coming round."

Let us suppose that a horse is ridden at a fence, A B (see Fig. 1), and that he "runs out" to the left; although the rider has pulled the animal's head round to the right, in his endeavour to keep him straight. In this case, the horse yielded to the rein with his neck, but refused to swing round his hind-quarters—a movement, on his part, which would have brought him at right angles to the fence (see Fig. 2); so that he would have had either to jump or to stop, neither of which actions would affect in any way the precision with which the turn had been made. Again, if a horse jibs in harness, and refuses to turn, say, to the right, we shall, in the vast majority of cases, have no difficulty in making him turn his head round in the required direction, although he will obstinately keep his hind-quarters fixed. The same may be said of a horse that rears. If these animals would only turn their hind-quarters round with the same facility that they bend their necks, they would lose their strongest "defence" against our "aids" (the reins and legs of the rider). It is evident that in every turn, the hind-quarters have to move round

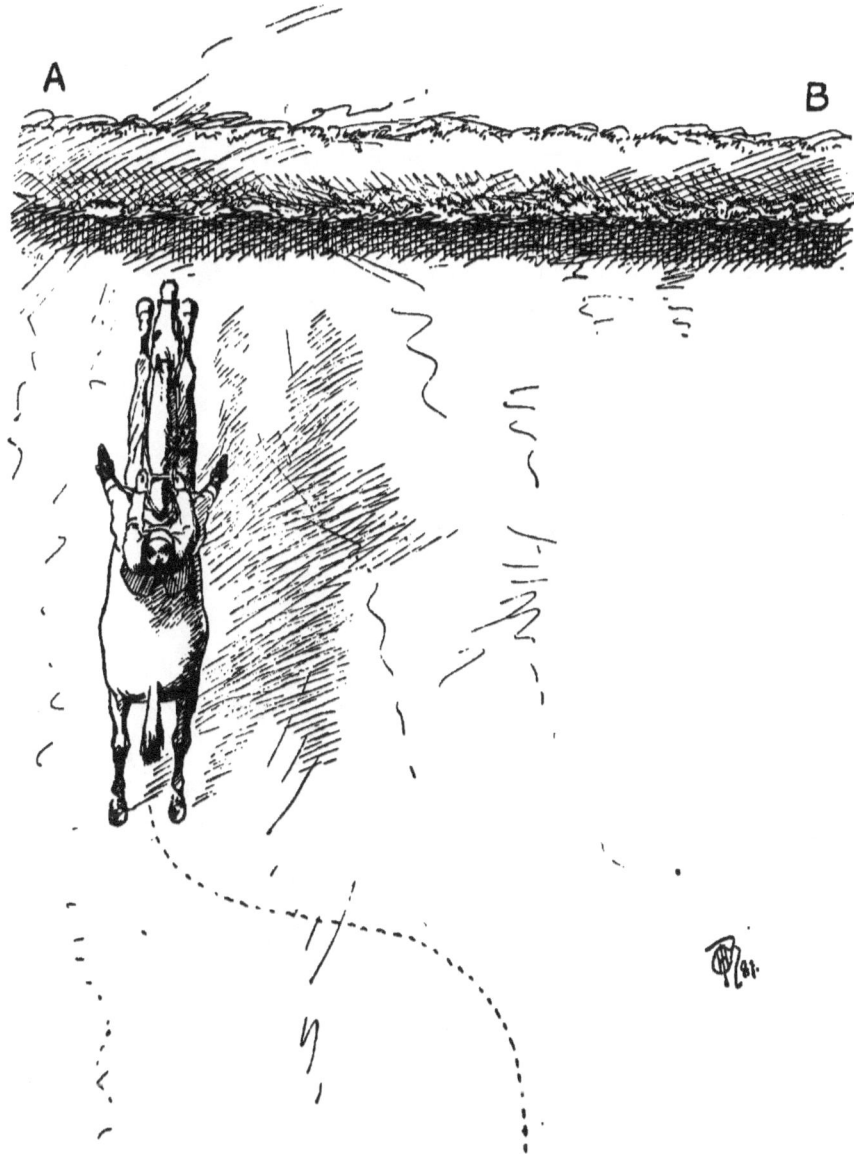

Fig. 2.—Shews horse having answered the pull of off rein as he should, and consequently coming straight at his fence.

in the opposite direction to the head and neck; the centre round which the movement is made, being advanced or brought back, according as the turn is made "on the forehand," or "on the haunches."

Reining back.—It is an axiom of the riding-school, worthy of implicit acceptance, that, until a horse has learned to rein back with facility and precision, he cannot be considered to have a good mouth; for, by performing this movement in the manner described, he shews that he is intelligently obedient to the indications of the rein, in yielding to its pressure, and, at the same time, in bringing his hind-legs "well under" him. Herein lies the value of the practice of reining back, which teaches the animal to understand that a pull on the reins is quite as much a signal for him to "collect" himself, as to moderate his pace. Hence, the use of a judicious pull when going at high "timber," or when galloping through heavy ground, especially, when the horse is tired. If, when travelling fast, the animal will only bend his neck to the rein, while letting his hindquarters sprawl out behind, he will quickly tire, and will, also, be a most unsafe "conveyance," from inability to raise his forehand, as occasion may require.

Lunging.—Although lunging usually forms a considerable portion of the work given to young horses, during their period of breaking, I mention it, here, solely with the object of advising its discontinuance altogether. Making a horse circle with the weight on his forehand, while his hind-quarters are "thrown out," not alone teaches him an awkward style of moving, but is also a fertile cause of sprain to the tendons and ligaments of the fore-limb. Again, as it is much more easy for the vast majority of men to keep turning round in one direction—in one opposite to that in which the hands of a clock revolve, for right-handed people—than in the other; it follows, that the generality of men, when they lunge a colt or filly, will circle the young one more to the left than to the right; just as we may see done any day on Newmarket Heath, opposite the railway station. The injurious effects of such a practice are self-evident. I shall describe, further on, a method of circling a horse—the breaker being on foot—by which the animal is made to move in a thoroughly "balanced" manner, and by which his mouth can be "formed" at the same time. I am confident that all good horsemen to whom it is new, will, on seeing how it is done, adopt it unreservedly. I am aware that the practice of lunging is discredited by many good breakers who are unacquainted with the method of circling which I have introduced.

Good hands.—The term "Good hands" signifies the ability of taking a pull at the rein—supposing it be required—when the horse's head is in the proper position for the mouth-piece to act on the "bars" of the animal's mouth; and of slackening them when the horse attempts to escape the pressure by bringing his head into a wrong position, or when the animal yields to the indication of the rein. The action of the mouth-piece, and the advisability of refraining from pulling at the reins when the head is in a wrong position, have been fully dealt with in the preceding pages. I may, however, draw attention to the fact that when the horse's head is in the wrong position for the action of the bridle, it is in an unfavourable one for the movements of the fore-limb; being raised or depressed to an undue extent, or too much flexed or extended on the neck (*i.e.* chin drawn in, or poked out). Hence, the natural tendency of the horse will be, if his mouth be not interfered with, to bring his head in the position which is the best for his own movements, and which is the most suitable for the action of the mouth-piece of the bridle. A hard-pulling horse, for instance, ridden or driven by a man with "good hands," will, probably, get his head "up," on feeling the pressure of the mouth-piece, when he tries to break away. Being inconvenienced in his movements by this awkward carriage of the head, and lacking, on account of the slackness of the reins, the incentive to keep it "up," he lowers it, to again experience the restraining pull. This will, probably, go on for a few times, until, wearied by a contest in which he finds himself baffled, he yields to the indication of the rein, and slackens his pace. Feeling that he "saves" his mouth the moment he does this, by the rider "giving" to him, he remains "in hand" for the rest of the journey. The typical "mutton-fisted" man, on the contrary, will keep hauling away at the reins, after the horse has got the mouth-piece on to the corners of the mouth, or, by getting his chin into his chest, and his head down, has transferred the pressure on to his poll. Consequently, the animal, experiencing the relief thus obtained, will naturally conclude that he has got the best of the battle, and will continue on his own course as long as he pleases. The harder such a man pulls on the reins, the more likely will he be to incite the animal to shew fight. In this case, the man foolishly pits the strength of his arms against the greatly superior power of the horse's neck. The rider with good hands, on the contrary, uses a pull on the reins, merely as a means of letting the animal know, that, if it will obey his wishes, it will "save" its own mouth; a hint which, as a rule, is readily taken. I need hardly say that the severer the bit, the better should be the hands of the man who employs it. A really fine horseman can ride with success in almost any kind of bit.

Snaffles and curbs.—The only advantage possessed by the curb over the snaffle is, as a rule, its greater power of control. This superiority is attended with the serious objections that: (1) the use of the curb is, often, irritating to the horse, who, if roused, can always successfully resist its control; and (2) that it is, more or less, detrimental to the action of the horse, by tending to make him averse from "going up to his bridle," and by obliging him, so as to "save" his mouth, to carry his head in a more or less constrained manner. As we can easily obtain the necessary control with the snaffle during breaking, it is evident that we should altogether dispense with the use of the curb during this process, so as to avoid the introduction of any disturbing element in the working out of the principle of using indications, rather than severity.

The thin, so-called, racing snaffle should not be used; as it is apt to wound the bars of the mouth, and thereby irritate the horse into shewing fight, which is the very thing we should seek to avoid while using the reins, of which, when we are in the saddle or driving seat, we are masters only on sufferance.

Elastic reins on dumb jockeys.—These contrivances should not be employed in breaking; for they never allow the complete freedom from pressure which the horse should experience as a reward for obedience, when he bends his neck and yields to the rein; unless, indeed, the elastic lines are ineffectually loose, or the animal draws in his head to an immoderate extent.

The standing martingale.—The use of this martingale is to prevent the horse from getting the mouth-

Fig. 3.—The proper length for a standing martingale.

piece off the bars, when he throws up his head.

Hence, if we employ it lengthened out, so that it will be just short enough to accomplish this object, and no more (see Fig. 3), it will give us the immense advantage of having the mouth-piece always in an effective position, with but little drawback. I, here, suppose that it is attached to the rings of the snaffle and not to the nose-band. At first glance, it may be considered that this mechanical restraint would be a constant source of danger, in the event of the animal getting into difficulties. I have frequently heard it urged,—but only by men who had not seen its use practically demonstrated,—that if a horse, on making a "blunder" at a fence, could not extend his head more than the properly lengthened out martingale would allow him to do, he would, being thus deprived of this supposed means of recovering his equilibrium, run a great risk of falling. We may see the fallacy of this argument, if we consider that the only effect of this poking out of the head, is to endanger the equilibrium, which becomes unstable, the moment a perpendicular line drawn through the centre of gravity, falls beyond the fore-feet. We find, therefore, by observing the comparative tightness, before and after jumping, of the standing martingale, that the horse's tendency, when fencing, is to bring his head back, on advancing the fore-limbs. If he adopts, with the martingale on, the other and unsafe course, the pain caused by the consequent severe pressure of the mouth-piece on the bars, will soon teach him to save his mouth by holding his head in a proper position. Besides the increased control obtained by the mouth-piece always remaining on the bars, the presence of the standing martingale, by stopping him from poking out his nose, will tend to prevent him going "uncollectedly" behind, and, even on this account alone, will be specially useful for the hunter, chaser, and polo pony. Whatever be the horse's work, whether on the flat, across country, or in harness, he should be ridden or driven in a standing martingale, if he has the habit of trying to get the mouth-piece off the bars of the mouth, or has any tendency to go uncollectedly. Objection to its use can be taken, only, in the case of the 'cross-country horse, who will be much more liable to be brought to grief by the practice of either of the faults just mentioned, than by this martingale. When he has learnt to carry himself properly, but not till then, should its employment be discontinued. Its constant use quickly teaches the horse to hold his head and to carry himself in the desired style; for obedience to the indications it automatically affords, is at once rewarded by relief to the mouth. No such useful lesson can be learned by the employment of the running martingale; for, with it, no saving of the mouth is obtained by any yielding of the head and neck to the rein. When it is on, whatever relief is procured, must be the result of the action of the rider's hands, which cannot possibly "give and take" with the same precision as the fixed martingale. I may mention, that this gear has the great advantage of preventing a rider with "bad hands," from hauling on the reins when the mouth-piece is on the corners of the mouth. Hence, the worse the rider, the more need he has of using a standing martingale with a horse that requires one.

That good horseman, Mr. Blew of *The Field*, remarks to me that he has seen one or two falls result from the use of the standing martingale, in cases of horses, out hunting, getting their fore-feet into a deep "gripe," and, then, being prevented by this gear, from throwing up the head, and, thus, relieving the fore-hand. He, consequently, advises that it should be employed, only, in breaking. Those fine steeplechase riders, Colonel Hickman of the 21st Hussars and Colonel Wardrop of the 12th Lancers, as well as many other good 'cross-country performers, consider, with me, that its addition renders horses requiring such restraint, safer over fences than they would be without it. Although the solution of this debatable question may be left to each man's own individual feeling on the matter, there can be no doubt as to its paramount importance in breaking, which is the subject, at present, before us.

The statement may be advanced, that men with really fine hands will gain nothing from the employment of the standing martingale. I entirely dissent from this; for it is impossible for any man, however delicate his touch may be, or strong his arms, to prevent, as this martingale will do, the animal from getting his head up, and thereby successfully resisting control, for the time being. I may mention that many of our finest Irish riders are its devoted admirers.

When a horse pulls hard, he will, almost invariably, try to advance his chin further than the standing martingale—at a proper length, let it be understood—will allow him to do. Hence, this amount of restraint will always be a direct saving to the arms; while it will be taken off the mouth, and the controlling indication afforded, the moment the animal brings his head back into its natural position. I need hardly explain, that the horse being unable to bring forward the bars of the lower jaw, will try, when resisting the action of the standing martingale, to advance his poll as much as possible, by bending the joint connecting the lower jaw to the head, and that by which the head is attached to the neck.

If the standing martingale be fixed on to the nose-band, it will fail to act in the manner described; owing to the fact that the pressure thus exerted on the nose by this strap, causes little or no pain; unless, indeed, it be specially arranged to produce this effect, as in the way described on page 217.

Nose-bands.—The use of the nose-band is to prevent the horse relieving the bars of some of the pressure of the mouth-piece, by opening his mouth; an action on his part which will tend to render this pressure oblique, and to transfer a portion of it to his poll.

CHAPTER III.

HORSE-CONTROL.

The breaking enclosure—Making a rope-halter—Haltering a loose horse—Making a loose horse stand still—Taking up a fore-leg—Holding up a fore-leg—Tying up a fore-leg—Blindfolding a horse—Applying the halter-twitch—The rope-twitch—The head-stall twitch—The bridle-twitch—The strait-jacket—Lifting up a hind-leg—Gagging a horse.

The breaking enclosure.—In order to carry out the system of breaking horses, it is a great advantage to have a proper enclosure, of about 20 yards square, with walls around it about 7 ft. high. The ground inside should be quite soft, so that horses which are made to lie down on it, may not run any chance of hurting themselves.

I may here impress on the reader the danger

there is to the breaker of having any one standing right behind him when he is handling vicious horses; for, in such a case, if the animal make an offensive movement, the man will probably knock up against the other, and thus fail to get out of harm's way.

Making a rope-halter.—The simplest way to do this is to take a half-inch rope, about 9 yards long; make it double for about 3 ft. 6 in.; put a knot on the doubled part, so as to form a large loop, in which make a small loop, for the leading rein to pass through. The second knot should divide the large loop, so that the head-piece should be about twice as long as the nose-band. The halter will now be ready to be put on (see Figs. 4 and 5). The nose-band may be made sufficiently long, and the loop through which the loose end passes, tight enough to prevent the nose-band and leading rein (the free end of the rope), forming a running noose, which might hurt the horse. Or, if required, a knot may be made with the leading rein at the ring through which

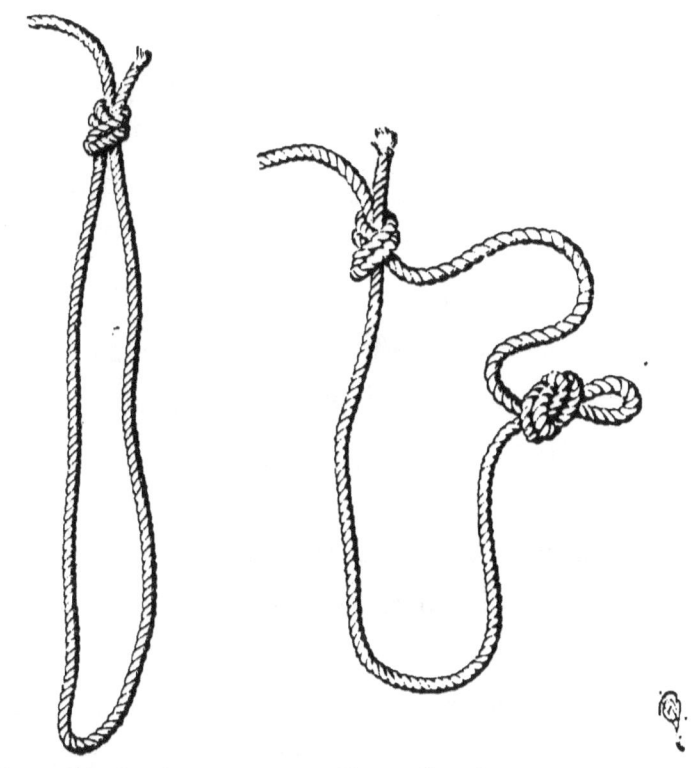

Fig. 4.—First loop in forming a rope-halter.

Fig. 5.—Second step.

it passes; so that the nose-band of the halter may not squeeze the horse's jaws together.

The rope employed should be soft, and not too thick, so as to allow the knots to be made with facility.

The reader will observe, that this halter which I have devised, is only an improvised adaptation, which need not take half a minute to make, of the ordinary rope-halter. I have no doubt that others, prompted by necessity, like myself, have hit on this rough-and-ready method; although I have never seen a halter made in quite the same manner as I have described.

Haltering a loose Horse.—Let us suppose that the animal is in some suitable enclosure, such as a yard, loose box, or small paddock; for it is almost needless to say, that if he were at liberty in the open, and averse from being captured, no man unaided could possibly catch him. The first thing to do is to make the rope-halter—as described in the preceding part of this chapter—if one be not at hand, and then to get the horse to stand quietly in some convenient corner. We may make him move, or stop, as may be required, by gently working a long pole held in the hands across the body, alternately, behind and in front of him; and, having got him into the proper position, we may induce him to stand steady, as I have found by experience, by touching him on the neck, and then rubbing it with the end of the pole. I have hardly ever known this to fail in its object. Horses, almost always, like having their necks scratched. As soon as the animal will stand still, while his neck is being "gentled" with the stick, the halter may be put on the end of the pole by a couple of turns (see Fig. 6), while the free end of the rope may be twisted once or twice round the pole, to prevent it hanging down too low. The operator will now take the pole, with the halter then rigged on to it, and will endeavour to bring the crown-piece of the halter behind the ears, without. frightening the animal; while holding the end of the pole a little above

G

its head (see Fig. 7). He can take the precautions I have described, for making the horse stand

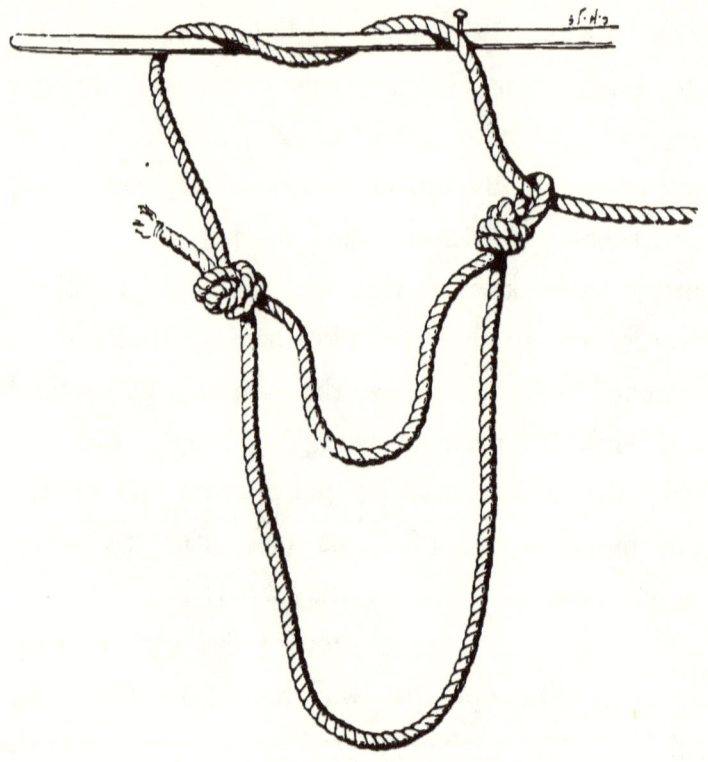

Fig. 6.—Rope-halter on pole, ready for use.

still, as he may think necessary. As soon as the crown-piece of the halter comes behind the ears,

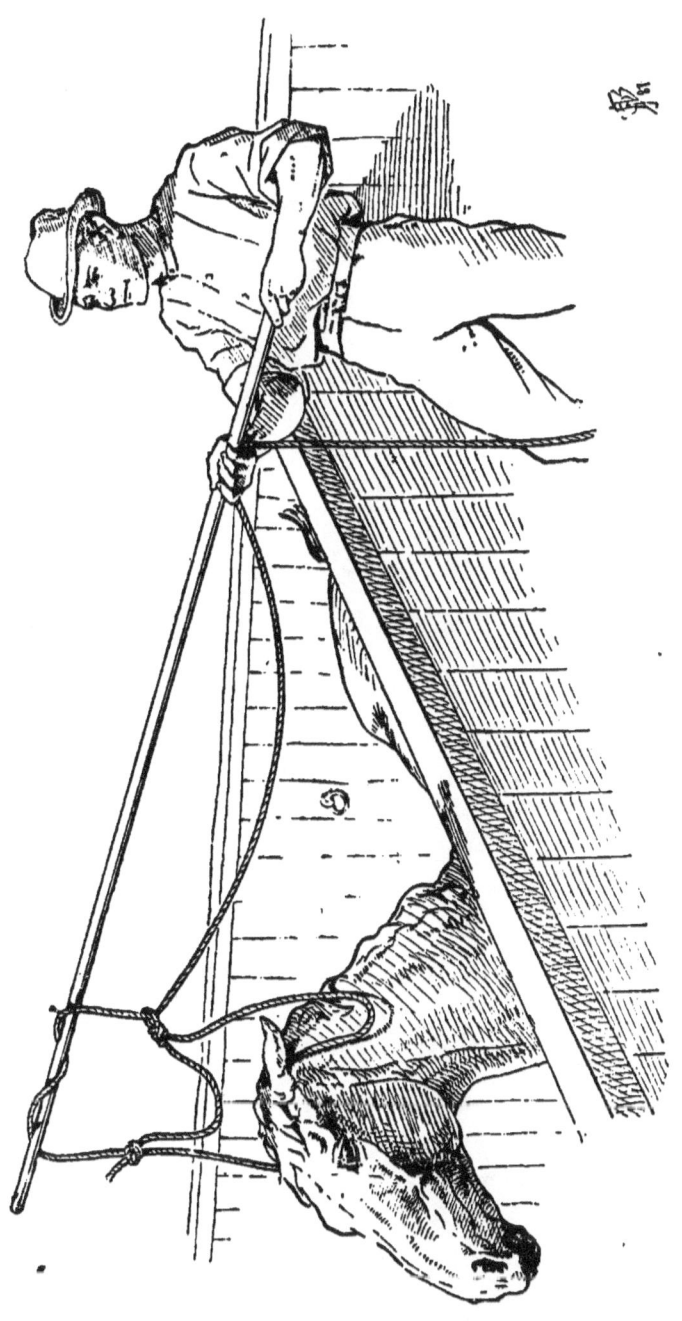

the operator should swing the pole smartly down in front of the animal's nose, and then under the lower jaw; a proceeding which will bring the halter into its proper place. Nothing now remains except to withdraw the pole. Care should be taken not to bring the pole under the lower jaw, until the nose-band is in front of the ears; for, if it remains behind them, when the end of the stick is brought down, the horse will be lassoed and not haltered. The precautions necessary to be taken in haltering the horse will depend on the amount of his vice, or timidity. A horse can be thus caught best, when he is standing in the corner of a wall which is too high for him to look over. In a circular enclosure, the animal will be able, by turning round, to defeat the intentions of his would-be captor, much more easily than he could do in a rectangular one. In a roped-in arena, the horse can get his head away from the halter, easier than he could do when close to a wall. There is no fear of a horse, however vicious he may be, of "charging home" on the operator, if the man keeps the pole across the animal's face, ready, if need be, to give him a tap or two on the muzzle. The larger the enclosure, the less will a horse attempt to "savage" any one approaching him. In extreme cases, a blow on the forehead might be necessary. I may mention that the brain is covered at the forehead, by only a thin plate of bone. Mr. O. S. Pratt, the American "horse-tamer," gives, in his book, a method for haltering a loose horse, by putting the crown-piece of the halter on the end of the pole (see Fig. 8). In applying this, the horse is very apt to shy away from the halter, which has to be put on from the front. The manner of haltering which I have described, and which was shewn to me by Mr. Banham, F.R.C.V.S., appears to be much better than Pratt's plan.

Making a loose Horse stand still.—If timidity

is the only cause that renders a loose horse difficult to halter, we may make him stand still after having put him in a proper enclosure, by

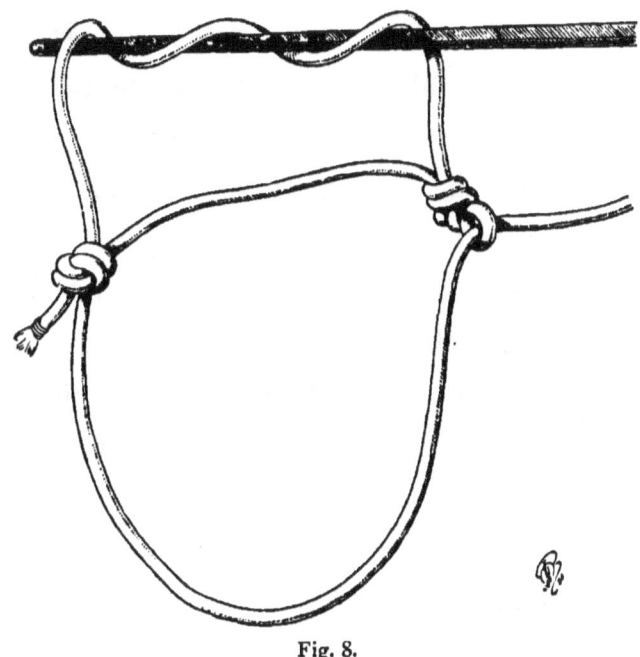

Fig. 8.

cutting him, with the whip, about the hocks and hind-heels whenever he attempts to turn round, and to shew his hind-quarters to the breaker. If the animal attempts to pass by, the man should stop him with the point of the whip. As soon as the horse understands that he exposes himself to punishment by turning round, he will, proportionately, abstain from doing so. He will then be readily induced to stand still by the point of the whip preventing him from passing; and the fear of punishment, from turning round. As a rule, the operator can quickly get up to his forehand by "gentling" his crest with the end of the whip or pole, and afterwards with the hand. The foregoing method, which I learned from that excellent teacher, Professor Sample, is not altogether suitable for horses that "strike out in front." The punishment that has to be inflicted during its application, may be an objection to its employment.

Taking up a fore-leg.—Having haltered the horse, we may, in order to gain further control over him, take up a fore-leg in two ways.

1. If we are afraid that the horse, on our approaching him, will "strike out," or kick, we

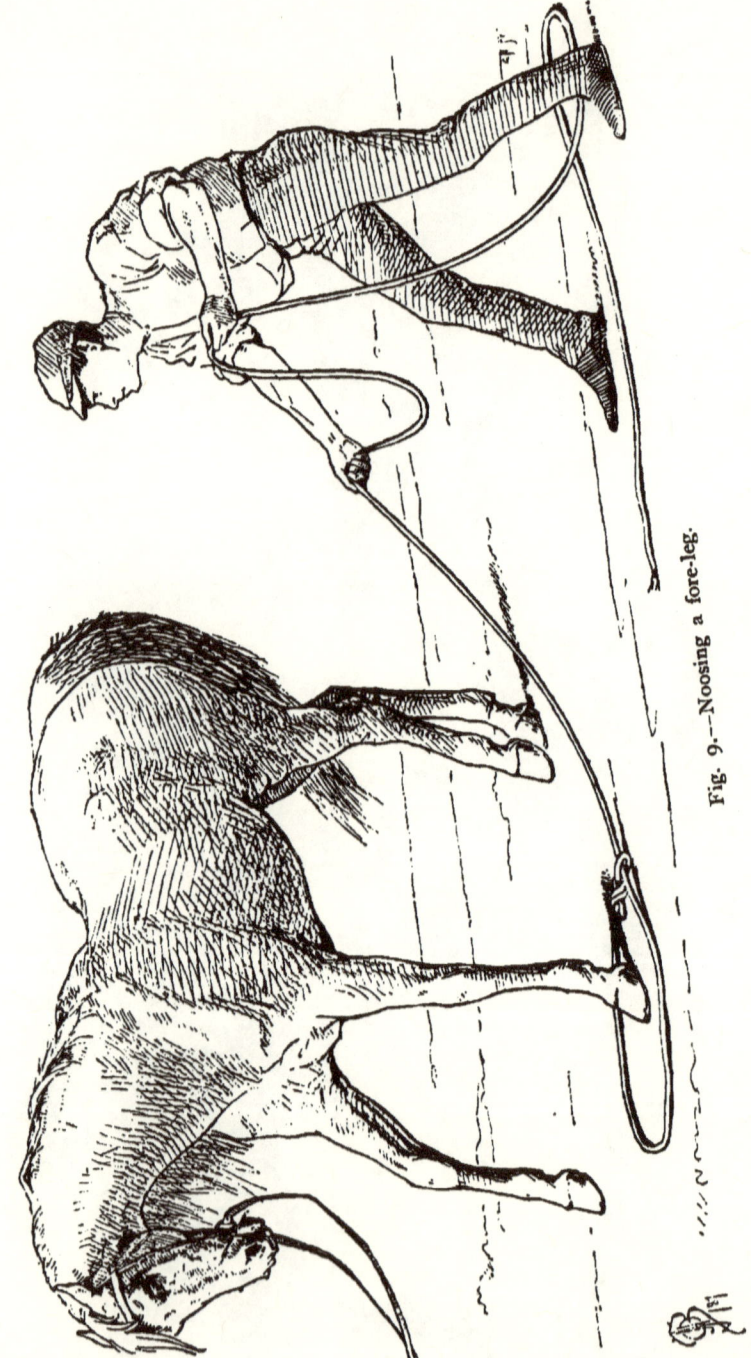

Fig. 9.—Noosing a fore-leg.

may, as Colonel Rawlins, R.H.A., shewed me, form a noose about two feet and a half in diameter, with a rope, and having laid it on the ground, give the free end to an assistant to hold. We may, then, make the horse move about until he places one fore-foot within the noose (see Fig. 9), when the assistant should pull the rope, and thus lasso the pastern. The end of the rope may, now, be thrown over the animal's back to the other side, and the leg pulled up (see Fig. 10); or, if the animal will not stand this being done, the leg may be pulled back by the rope, and lifted up by another assistant. If the horse "shews fight," it may be necessary to blindfold him at this stage of the proceedings. The long pole may, also, be called into requisition to "gentle" the horse, and thus render him comparatively quiet. The operator can always quickly accomplish his object, in the manner described, if he will only exercise a little patience.

I may mention that this method of noosing the leg, is precisely similar to that employed in securing the limbs of wild elephants, in India, when they have been driven into a stockade.

2. The best way for lifting up a fore-leg, with the hand, is, as I have found out, to grasp, say, the near fore, with the left hand; pinch it with the fingers to stimulate the flexors of the knee to contract; turn the elbow in, and press it against the upper part of the fore-arm, so as to throw the weight from the near, on to the off fore, and thus to render the picking-up of the near fore a very easy matter (see Fig. 11). If required, an upward pull is given with the left arm, and the foot is caught with the right hand as the horse lifts it up. I may add, that the muscles against which the man's elbow presses assist in raising the foot from the ground. By this plan the breaker can stand at the side of the leg that has to be raised, and a little away from it, thus keeping out of danger, as much as possible. If

PICKING UP A FORE-LEG. 95

he attempts to lift the fore-leg of a bad cow-kicker, in the ordinary way, by catching hold of

Fig. 11.—Picking up a fore-leg.

the pastern, he will run a great risk of getting hit

on the head or body, by having to stoop down while standing close to, and a little behind, the fore-leg.

Mr. J. Leach, M.R.C.V.S., shewed me a neat method for lifting up the leg of a heavy cart-horse, by catching the hair of the fetlock, and then drawing up the leg. The slight irritation caused by the pull at the roots of the hair will cause the horse to readily bend the knee.

Holding up a fore-leg.—If the fore-leg be held up by the hand passing under the fetlock or pastern, as is frequently done, the horse, by bearing a portion of his weight on the man's hand, can easily kick with either hind-leg. The foot should, on the contrary, be held by the hoof, under which the fingers pass, while the thumb presses down on the sole (see Fig. 12). The animal will now avoid placing weight on the man's hand; for by doing so he would cause the joints of the foot to become bent in a painful manner.

Fig. 12.—How to hold up a fore-leg.

A convenient way for holding up the fore-leg, for "gentling" and other purposes, is that shewn by Fig. 10.

Tying up a fore-leg.—Having "picked up" the foot, we may secure it as follows:

1. By Rarey's leg strap, which is about 3 ft. long, and is furnished, at one end, with a buckle, below which, a leather "keeper" is placed on both sides (see Fig. 13). To apply it, the free end is passed round the pastern, from the outside, through the keeper at the back of the buckle, thus forming a loop. Another turn is taken round the forearm, and a second loop is made by passing the end through the buckle. The strap can now be tightened up as may be required, and the end run through the second keeper. Fig. 14 shews how this can be equally well done with a stirrup leather, with which two or three turns have been taken round the pastern; so as to bring the punched holes sufficiently near

the buckle. (See, also, Fig. 16.) The objections to the employment of this method of tying up the leg are: (*a*) That it is apt to irritate the animal

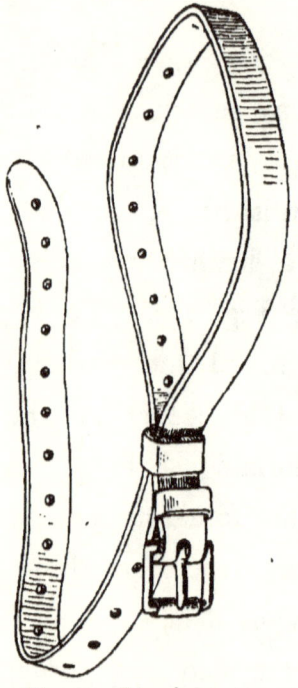

Fig. 13.—Rarey's leg-strap.

by the compression needed to keep the strap in its place; (*b*) That, when the leg is thus fixed, the horse, in the event of his "coming down," is liable to hurt his knee, "capped knee" being the usual result of the injury; on account

Fig. 14.—Tying up fore-leg with stirrup-leather.

of the broad extensor tendon being, necessarily, tightly stretched over the part. I have had this accident occur, on different occasions, when making a horse lie down, even when he had knee-caps on, and when the ground was quite soft; (*c*) The heel of the shoe, if one be on, is apt to bruise and cut the elbow; (*d*) The compression exercised by the strap on the fore-arm numbs the leg, and tends to make the animal fall awkwardly, if he is made to lie down; (*e*) Unless the strap is kept very tight, it is apt to slip down the fore-arm, and thus exercise an injurious strain on the fetlock joint.

2. By far the best way for tying up a fore-leg is the one described by Mr. Saunders in 'Our Horses,' by which the leg is simply suspended, at any length required, from the surcingle. Mr. Saunders advises the use of a small loop to connect the surcingle and strap together (see Fig. 15), with the object, I presume, of keeping the limb in a plane parallel to the general direction of the horse's body. This is certainly an advantage when making a horse lie down, although I have found, for ordinary purposes of control,

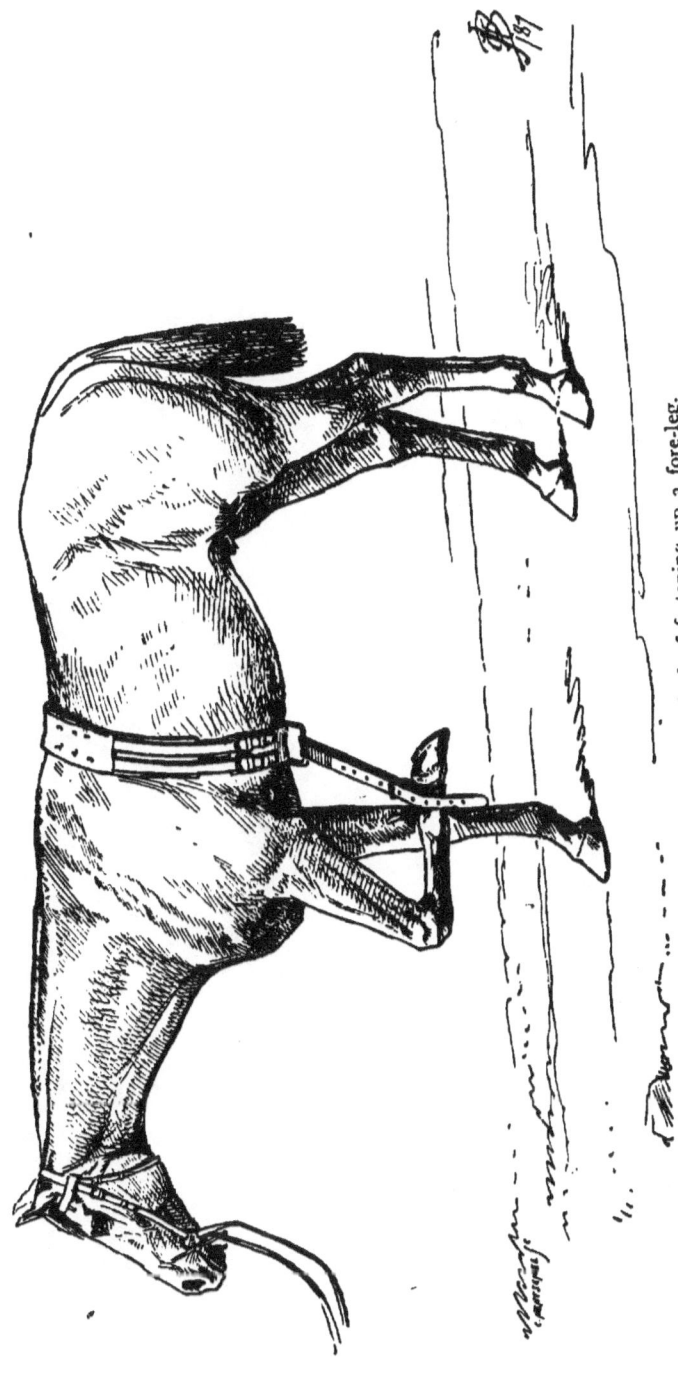

Fig. 15.—The best method of fastening up a fore-leg.

that the employment of the small loop may be dispensed with, and the leg-strap passed through the surcingle, or girth.

This method of suspending the leg is most useful, when gentling the fore-limb, and when shoeing a "difficult" animal ; as the foot can be retained at any convenient height from the ground without irritating the horse, and, consequently, without inciting him to "fight."

I have learned, on more than one occasion, by bitter experience, that it is possible for a horse to effectually cow-kick with the hind-leg of the side on which a fore-leg is tied up.

A stirrup leather, with two or three holes punched at convenient distances, will make a capital leg-strap (see Fig. 16). It has the advantage of having, at the back of the buckle, no leather keeper, which is always liable to give way, by reason of the strain exerted on it.

For suspending a fore-leg, we need punch no extra holes in the leather, if we take, as before described, a few turns with it round the pastern, before passing its end through the lower part of

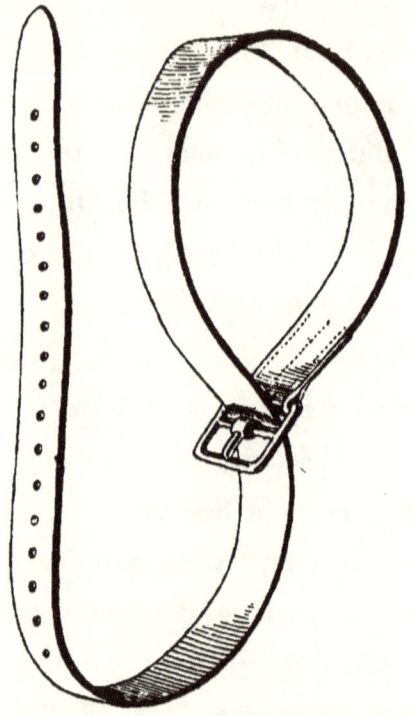

Fig. 16.—A stirrup leather as used for holding up a fore-leg.

the buckle. This way would naturally take a few seconds longer than if the holes were punched at proper distances, and, consequently, is not as applicable as the other, to horses that are extremely difficult to handle.

Blindfolding a Horse.—After the animal has been secured in the manner described, or after he has been simply haltered, a further step in the process of rendering him helpless may be taken, by throwing a rug, or other convenient cloth, over his head, and then applying the rope-twitch (see page 113). If he be dangerous to approach, the rug may be placed on the end of a long pole, and then brought over his head, or a blindfolding halter may be put on, now, or in the first instance. The originating idea of this appliance is, I believe, of French origin. It consists of an ordinary halter, with a cloth filling up the space between the cheek-pieces, brow-band, and nose-band; so as to cover the horse's eyes.

Blindfolding is an efficient means of control with the majority of horses, although it excites some to offer more vigorous resistance than they would otherwise do. I have never found a horse that would, when blindfolded, attempt to kick, or strike out, on the chance of hitting his man, unless he was touched about the limbs or body; nor bite, whether touched or not, under similar circumstances. I, therefore, think that the breaker runs no risk whatsoever in going up to the animal's head, when it is, thus, temporarily deprived of sight, no matter how vicious it may be.

Applying the halter-twitch.—At this stage of the proceedings, the breaker may apply a modification of Pratt's twitch, by making a half hitch with the free part of the rope of the halter, passing the loop over the ears (see Fig. 17), bringing the lower part of the loop under the animal's upper lip, and then pulling it taut (see Fig. 18). He may jerk the rope (leading rein) three or four times, accompanying the action on each occasion with the word "steady." I may mention that the part of the rope which passes

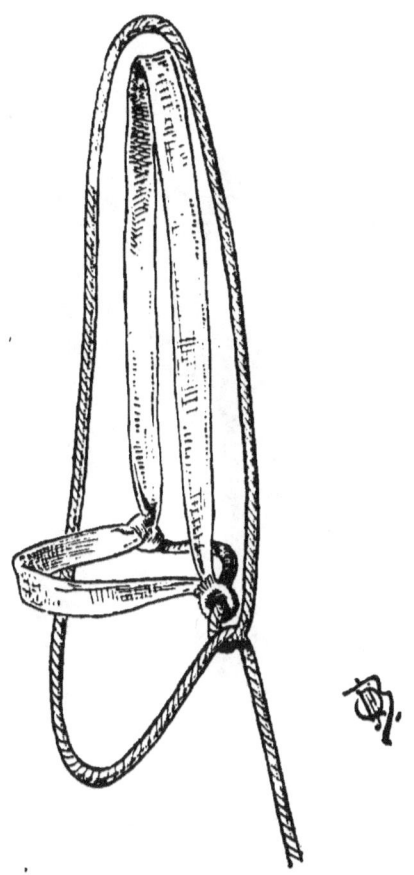

Fig. 17.—The halter-twitch.

under the upper lip, should be kept slack, except

when the jerk is given, and that any other

Fig. 18.

suitable word may be substituted for that of "steady." It is now perfectly safe to remove the blindfolding apparatus; as no horse will attempt any aggressive movement towards the man who holds the leading rein, when thus secured. The rope may be jerked and the word "steady" used, as may be required. The pain inflicted by the application of this twitch, is a necessary evil, which may well be disregarded; for its amount is trifling in comparison with the extent of control obtained by its means. If employed carefully, no mark need be left on the mucous membrane. The proper use of this twitch is thoroughly rational, for it keeps the horse quiet by its deterrent effect, and not by retaining the horse in a continued state of suffering, as is done by the ordinary twitch. The word "steady," or any convenient substitute for it, should never be omitted; for, after the animal has learned, as he will do in a minute or two, to connect it with the idea of pain, the twitch may be removed, and the word alone used, in order to keep him in subjection. In this experiment, it is evident that the horse fears the word, and not the twitch; for, no matter how often the rope is put on, he will not resent its application more than he did on the first occasion. The oftener, on the contrary, the ordinary twitch is employed, the shyer will the animal become of having his muzzle touched. The chief advantages of the rope-twitch over the common one, are: that it can be easier procured and applied; it does not inflict so much pain, which, with it, is momentary, and not continuous, as with the other; it is more effective; it is not so liable to slip off; it can be retained in position for any reasonable length of time, to be used as required; it has a more or less permanently good effect on the horse's temper, and not a bad one, like the other; and it does not make the horse shy of having his mouth touched. The fact of numbers of horses being rendered difficult to bridle, by the employment of the ordinary twitch, will, naturally, occur to the reader. The general substitution of this twitch for the ordinary one, by veterinary surgeons, would certainly remove a grave reproach against us which now exists. It is, of course, used by them, only, *faute de mieux*.

If, when the ordinary twitch is twisted up tight, its stick be struck or jerked, as some do, on the animal moving, it will doubtless have a deterrent effect, as well as the one produced by the brutal and needless infliction of continued pain.

The rope-twitch. — Everything I have said in the preceding paragraphs, respecting the halter-twitch, applies equally well to its original form, as described in Mr. O. S. Pratt's book, 'The Horse's Friend,' which was published at Buffalo in 1876. Mr. C. G. Frasier, who was Pratt's assistant for some years, in America, tells me, that this twitch was not invented by Pratt, long before whose time it was in use. He thinks that it was, probably, the idea of the "horse-tamer,"

Fanchion, who practised his art many years ago in the States. Pratt calls it "the double-hitch Bonaparte bridle." It is made as follows: Take

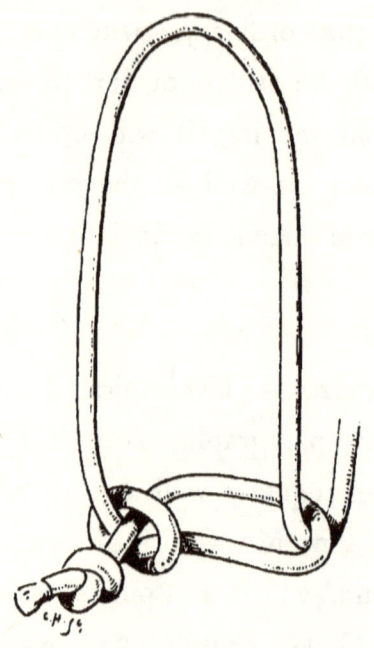

Fig. 19.—Pratt's rope-twitch, first portion.

a rope, and make a simple knot with it at one end, at a distance of about eighteen inches from which make another knot loosely, and pass the first knot through the second, so as to form a

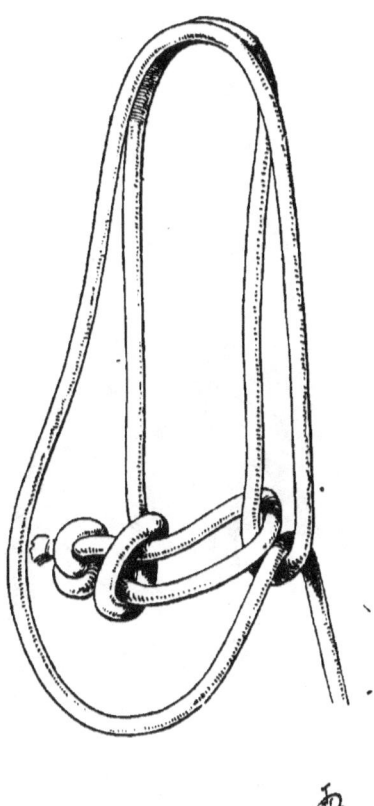

Fig. 20.—Pratt's twitch completed.

loop which will not draw tight. Make a halter

by taking a turn of the rope through the fixed loop (see Fig. 19). Place the halter over the horse's head, and the loop in his mouth. Make a half hitch with the free part of the rope, pass

Fig. 21.—Pratt's twitch on horse's head, and tightened at word "steady."

it over the horse's head and under his upper lip, and draw moderately tight (see Figs. 20 and 21). By making the fixed loop long, one can obtain more power than with the halter-twitch.

If an ordinary head-stall or snaffle-bridle is on, the twitch may be applied by knotting the end of the rope to one of the D's on the cheek-pieces of the former, or to one of the rings of the latter,

Fig. 22.—Head-stall twitch on horse.

and passing the half hitch over the ears and under the upper lip, as before described.

If there be much difficulty in applying the rope-twitch, the horse may be tied head and tail (see page 197), and it can then be put on without trouble; the animal being, of course, released, immediately after this is done.

Head-stall twitch.—Fig. 22 will explain this ready and effective method of applying the twitch. The rope is passed through the upper ring of the cheek-piece of the head-stall, and is tied on to the lower ring. The turn over the ears and under the upper lip is, then, taken, with the portion of rope which, after being drawn out, is included between the two rings.

The bridle-twitch.—This is a useful and ready means for making the horse stand quiet after he is bridled, and is applied by passing one of the snaffle-reins under the upper lip, and drawing it tight to the opposite side (see Figs. 23 and 24). I was shewn this twitch by Mr. Esa, of the firm of Shaikh Ibrahim & Co., Poona.

The strait-jacket.—For English readers, I

venture to apply this term to the *hippo lasso*

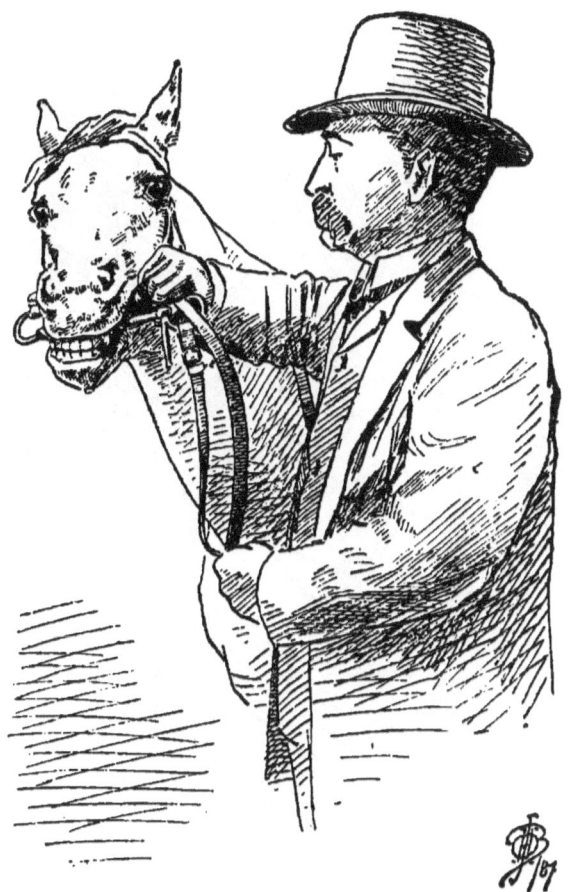

Fig. 23.—The bridle-twitch, front and near-side view.

of MM. Raabe and Lunel. It consists of a

breachen and breast-band, supported by straps

Fig. 24.—The bridle-twitch, off-side view.

passing over the back, and connected by traces,

which proceed from the breachen, through D's, with rollers on them, at the end of the breast-band, back again through similar D's on the breachen, and then forward; to become finally attached to buckles on the sides of the breast-band (see Fig. 25). A strap and buckle, laid along the top of the back, connects the two back straps together. A felt guard may be used with the supporting strap of the breast-band, so as to prevent it hurting the back. The breachen should be lined with felt. The back straps should be made of strong stirrup leather. The traces should be particularly strong, close to the breachen. The breachen and breast-band should be provided, at their respective centres, with a D, to which ropes may be attached, in order to keep the animal steady, before and behind.

This gear may be applied in the following way:

If the horse is quiet, the breast-band and breachen may be put on separately, with the back straps supporting them, and may be connected together by the strap on the top of the

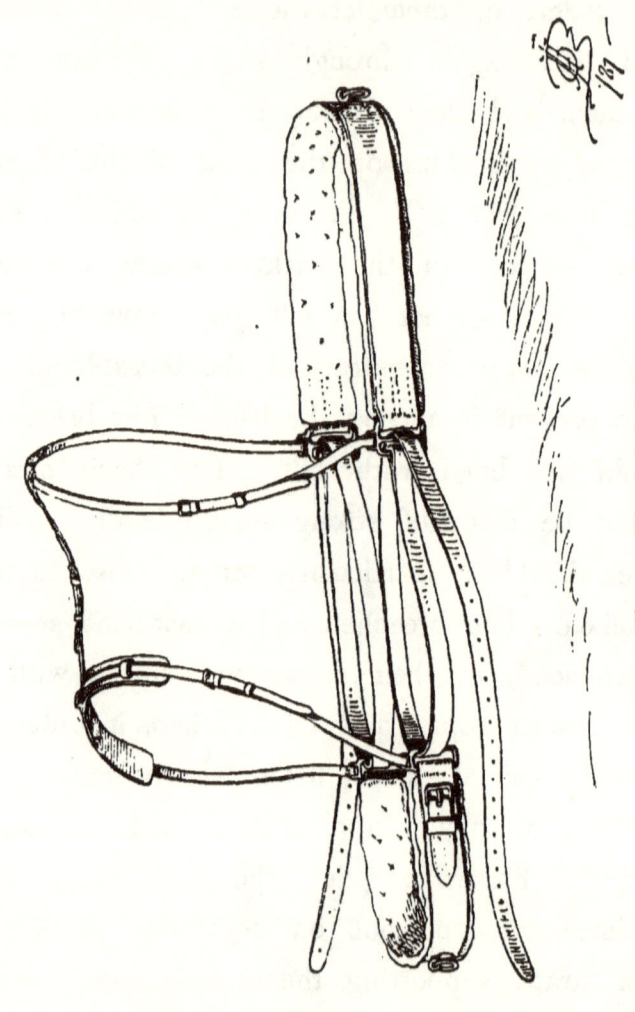

Fig. 25.—The strait-jacket.

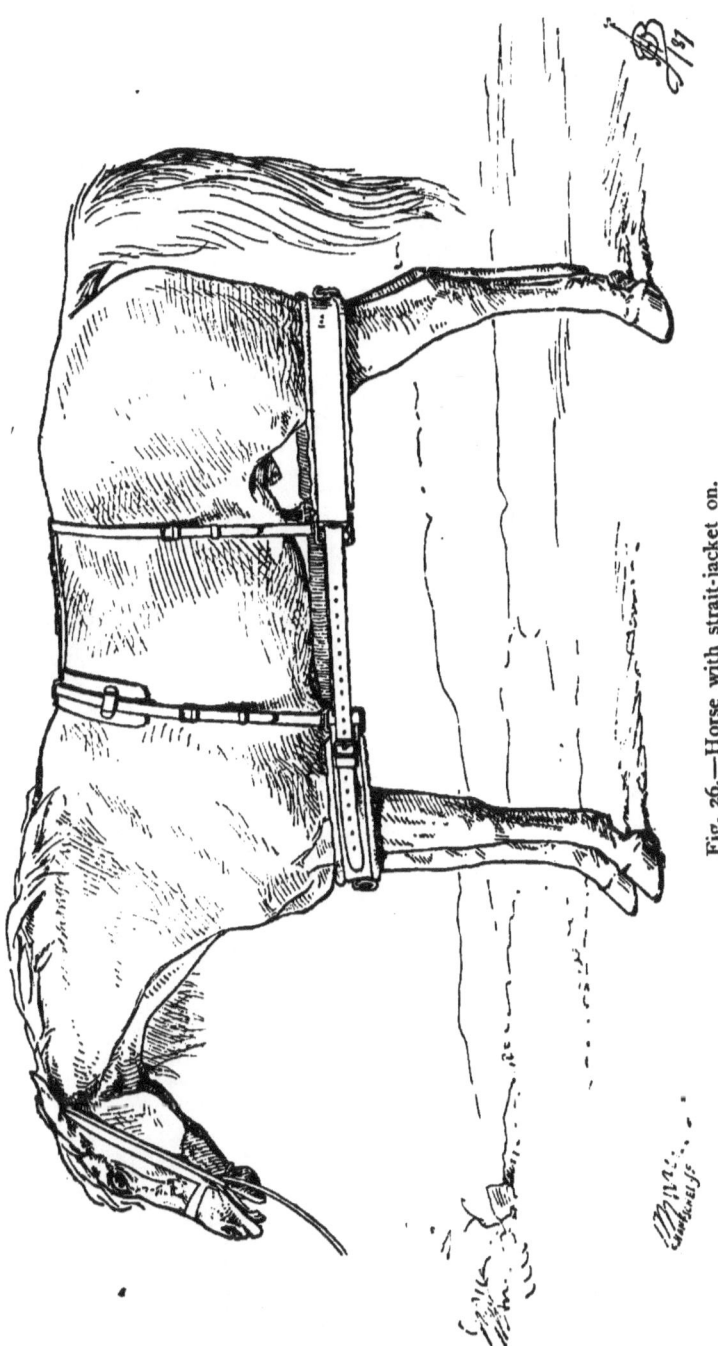

Fig. 26.—Horse with strait-jacket on.

back, and by the traces on each side. The breast-band should rest high up against the forearms, and the breachen behind, and a little below the level of the stifles (see Fig. 26).

If the animal is dangerous to handle, only, behind; the breast-band may be put on, and the breachen attached to it, in the manner just described, but without putting it over the quarters. A rope can now be fixed to the D in the centre of the breachen, which, by the aid of the rope, can be pulled over the croup into its proper position, by an assistant from behind. Before doing this, the traces should be let out, to be pulled tight, the moment the breachen slips over the tail. In this and other cases of difficulty, ropes may be attached to the ends of the traces, so that the assistants who hold them, need run no risk of getting kicked.

When the horse strikes out, as well as kicks, the different parts of the strait-jacket may be connected together, with the exception of, say, the near trace, the end of which may be held by an assistant, while another helper holds a rope attached to the D which is on the near side of the breast-band. The loop formed by the breast-band and its back strap is, now, passed over the horse's neck, the end of the near trace passed through the near side D of the breast-band, and the remaining fixings accomplished. Or, if the animal be not very violent, the gear may be connected together; the loop made by the breast-band and its back strap, passed over the head and neck; and the breachen pulled over the croup by a rope.

If the precaution of putting on the rope-twitch be taken, no difficulty need be experienced in subsequently applying the strait-jacket.

Lifting up a hind-leg.—The two methods to which I need direct my readers' attention, for performing this operation, are as follows:

1. If the operator has two assistants—one to

Fig. 27.—Picking up a hind-leg.

K

Fig. 28.—First step in picking up a hind-leg without the assistance of a helper.

hold the horse, the other to hold up, say, the near fore-leg—he may get alongside the animal's near hind; catch the *tendo Achillis* (the hamstring) with the left hand, and the pastern, backhanded, with the right hand; give a signal to the assistant to let go the near fore; then lift the leg, and place it resting on his left thigh (see Fig. 27).

If he has no one to hold up the near fore, he may "pick it up" in the way previously described; grasp the hoof with the right hand, while facing to the horse's rear (see Fig. 28); take a step forward with the left foot; catch the hamstring with the left hand (see Fig. 29); let go the near fore, and, at the same moment, seize the pastern, backhanded, with the right hand; and place, as before, the animal's leg on the left thigh. This method, which, I believe, I have been the first to devise, ensures almost complete immunity from danger. As long as one has hold of the fore-hoof with the hand, one can get forward, out of danger, if the horse tries to kick. The grasp of the left hand deprives the hind-leg of the greater part of its action, and the hind pastern is caught so quickly after, even if not before, the near fore reaches the ground, that the animal has not time to make a deliberately offensive movement. By catching the pastern in the way described, we aid in preventing the animal from cow-kicking, to do which, he must bend his hock; for the muscle which flexes the foot extends the hock. Were we to catch the canon bone, instead of the pastern, we should, besides losing this advantage, have less ability to act on the lever formed by the bones below the hock, by reason of our shifting the point of application of the "power," closer to the fulcrum (the head of the *tibia*). The irritation caused by the grasp of the hand on the hamstring—which is composed of two tendons—stimulates their muscles to contract, and, thus, to keep the hock extended. In this operation, we should follow the principles, already laid down, of removing the cause of any pain or irritation,

inflicted by us on the horse, the moment he yields to our wishes. I need hardly say, that if the horse overpowers the grip of our hands on his hind-leg, and kicks out behind, he can do us no harm, for we are then in front of his hind-leg. If the animal will not submit, we should apply the rope-twitch (see page 113); and, by its aid, and a little "gentling," proceed as before described.

2. In order to "gentle" the hind limb, or to take it up and let it down at will, while maintaining complete control over it, we may proceed as follows: Put on, say, the near hind pastern, a hobble with a D attached to it. Take a strong cord about 20 ft. long, and tie with it a "double sheet bend" (see Fig. 30) to the end of the tail, in the middle of the cord. Pass one end through the D to the near side, the other end through it to the off side, and give the respective ends to an assistant on each side to hold (see Fig. 31). These men should stand at right angles to the horse, and can lift the leg by

pulling equally on their respective cords. In this

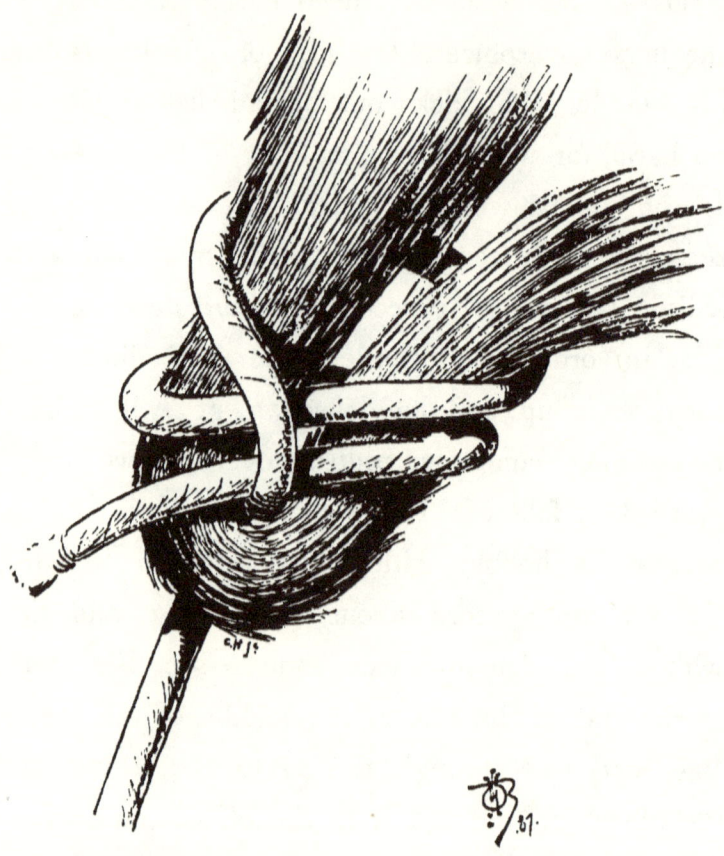

Fig. 30.—Shewing how to fasten a rope to the end of horse's tail with a "double sheet bend."

manner, the leg will be brought straight up under

the body, so as not to throw the animal off his balance. The fact of thus keeping the joints of the leg flexed will obviate any chance of his

Fig. 32.—Leg pulled back with one rope, a method which should be avoided; as it throws the horse off his balance.

straining himself while struggling, which he might do by the old method of using only one cord, which will necessitate the leg being pulled back,

Fig. 33.—Mode of fastening a rope to a short tail.

and will, consequently, disturb the animal's equili-

Fig. 34.

brium (see Fig. 32). By the other and better method, which was taught me by Colonel W. Gatacre, the foot may be lifted up, and put down again, without causing the animal any inconvenience. It is a most valuable means for "gentling" the hind limb; for its action is irresistible, and, at the same time, causes no irritation. If the horse's tail is too short to make a knot in its hair, we may pass a loop made in the middle of a doubled cord over the dock, and further secure it by a half hitch (Figs. 33 and 34).

I have devised the following method for improvising a hobble for lifting up a hind-leg, which, I think, will be found useful. Place a stirrup iron, foot part pointing to the rear, at the back of the hind pastern; take a few turns, with the stirrup-leather, round the pastern and iron, and buckle up (Fig. 35).

Gagging a Horse.—This is useful for preventing the animal using his teeth aggressively, and, also,

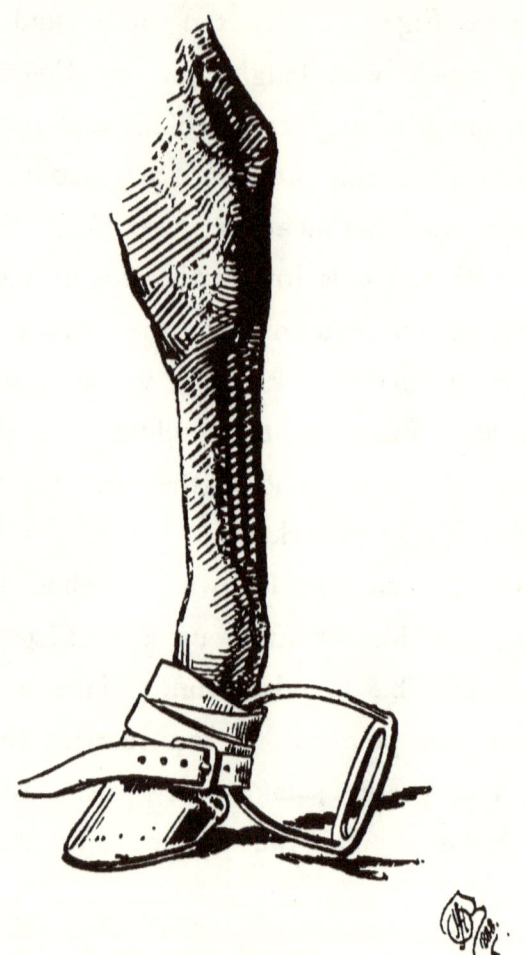

Fig. 35.—Improvised hobble made with a stirrup iron.

for breaking him of this objectionable habit. The

one I use is made out of a block of hard wood, 5 inches long and 2 inches square, which is made octagonal by planing off the corners. Lately, I have had this gag made with a semicircular groove, about a third of an inch broad, running

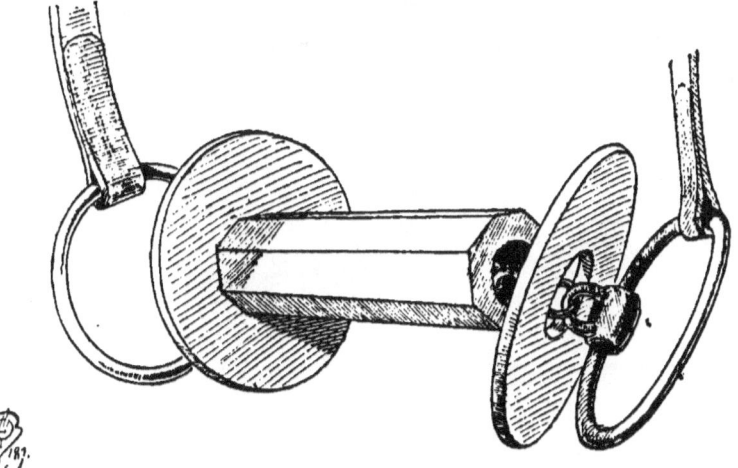

Fig. 36.—Wooden gag.

down the centre of each face of the octagonal, in order to make it more "punishing." A hole is bored, down the centre, for a chain which is attached to the head-stall. I use leather guards on each side to prevent the animal from getting

L

the gag out of his mouth (see Fig. 36). This is a modification of Rarey's wooden mouthing bit, which was a round block of wood.

General Peat suggested to me the advisability of having the gag made with sharp edges, and not round; so as to teach the horse, by the pain inflicted on his gums, not to bite.

CHAPTER IV.

RENDERING HORSES DOCILE.

The crupper leading rein—Gentling the horse—Throwing the horse with the strait-jacket—Making the horse lie down by means of the cord—Keeping the horse in a constrained position on the ground.

IN this chapter, we need consider only quick methods of removing a horse's nervousness, and proving to him that he need have no fear of us, or of his other surroundings; for the ordinary ways of accustoming him to the presence of man, are too self-evident to need any special mention here. The breaker, however, should remember that, by adopting a system of "gentling," which requires several days, if not weeks, for its completion, he runs the risk of allowing the horse to find out his own power of resistance—a species of knowledge which our rapid style of breaking never permits him to acquire. If the animal sulks, or exhibits deliberate impatience of control, he should be conquered, then and there, as I have mentioned on page 11.

The crupper leading-rein.—Whichever style of breaking be adopted, the first step that I would advise, is to accustom the horse to the "crupper leading-rein," which can be readily made by taking a long rope, doubling it, making a loop in the middle by knotting it, and passing the loop under the horse's tail, and the ends of the rope through the halter, or rings of the snaffle (see Fig. 37). By using this leading-rein in preference to one attached to the head-stall or halter, the animal will never attempt to "hang on" the leading-rein, as he will often do with the other, and, when led, instead of "going on his fore-hand," will move, as he ought to do, "collectedly," on

Fig. 37.

account of the pressure of the rope making him "bring his hind-quarters well under him." I do not know who invented this form of crupper, which was known to Fanchion, Magner, Pratt, Rockwell, and all the other American "horse-tamers."

Gentling the Horse.—Having put on this crupper leading-rein, the horse may be gentled all over with a long pole. We may, then, lift up his fore and hind legs, successively, and handle him all over. Every display of confidence on his part should be rewarded by encouraging words, patting, and, if procurable, a piece of carrot, or, if he will eat it, a bit of bread, or lump of sugar. If we have got a strait-jacket at hand, we may use it with advantage, in the event of his proving very nervous. If the horse shews fight, we may employ the gag and rope-twitch, invariably using, with the latter, the word "steady," and discontinuing the application of the rope as soon as the animal obeys the word.

Throwing the Horse with the strait-jacket.— If we want to produce a stronger, or different effect, we may make the horse lie down by means of the strait-jacket. To do this, one assistant should stand at his head, another should hold a rope attached to his tail, so that he may not throw himself forward on to his mouth; while an assistant at each of the traces should pull them tight, and thus bring him down. As soon as he is on the ground, he should be gentled and handled, all over, for a few minutes. The process may be repeated, or lengthened, as may be required. If, say, the off-trace be tightened up and buckled, the aid of the assistant, who would otherwise have held this trace, may be dispensed with. This method of throwing the horse is the gentlest in its action of any I have ever seen. If the appliances and help be at hand, and the breaker be not pressed for time, I would recommend that this method of throwing should be always used, as a preliminary to that of making a horse lie down by pulling his head round, which I shall presently describe; so as to take some of the "fight" out of him, and to prevent him, as much as possible, from "knocking himself about."

Making the Horse lie down by means of the cord.—If the horse refuses to give in, we may make him lie down in the following manner, which Professor Sample informs me was invented by the American "horse-tamer," Hamilton. It is a modified and greatly improved form of Rarey's method. Place on the horse, a surcingle which has three rings on its pad, and attach a crupper to the rearmost ring. Tie a rope to the tail for an assistant to hold; so as to be able to pull the horse over, on the proper side, if he appears likely to fall the wrong way. Put on the horse's head, a leather head-stall, having a circular D on one side, or attach an iron ring to the D, so that the cord which has to be employed, may run smoothly through it. Fix a strong cord to the middle ring on the pad; pass it through the ring on the side of the head-stall, and back through the front ring on the pad. Put knee-caps on, and suspend to the surcingle the fore-leg of the side, away from which the head will be turned (see Fig. 38). The buckle of the leg-strap should be put on the inside, so that when the horse lies on his off side, there may be no difficulty in undoing the strap, in order to let him up. Then, all being ready, take the end of the cord, draw the head round, say, to the near side, bring the cord across the base of the neck, and pull on it from the off side, until the animal yields, and rolls over on to that side. When the horse goes down, comparatively, easily, the free part of the cord may be drawn over his back, as in Fig. 38, and not under his neck. No attempt should be made to throw him forcibly down; for the effect we should aim at is that produced by his "giving in" to power which he finds irresistible. Hence, the more he fights, and

Fig. 38.—Throwing a horse by means or pulling his head round with a rope

pits the strength of his muscles against the action of our mechanical appliances, the better will be the result. If the horse appears likely to fall on his near side, the assistant who holds the rope should pull him over on to his off side; for, if he fell on the near side, he would be in the awkward position of having his neck doubled under him. The horse may now be kept, say ten minutes, on the ground, with his head pulled round to his side (see Fig. 38), and "gentled." When "gentling" the horse on the ground, the breaker should remain at his back, so as to keep out of reach of his heels.

Having carefully attached a rope-noose to the off hind pastern, the breaker may pull that hind limb toward himself, and gentle it.

I need hardly say that it is quite immaterial to which side the horse's head is drawn, provided that, in either case, the opposite leg be tied up.

Keeping a horse in a constrained position on the

ground.—If the animal goes down without a struggle, and sulks on the ground, he should be forced to "shew fight" by keeping him in the constrained position depicted in Fig. 39, until he has got rid of the most of his "temper" by ineffectual struggling. When a horse begins to groan, and to considerably moderate the violence of his struggles, we may feel confident that "the sulk" has been taken out of him, more or less, and that he is fit to be allowed to get on to his feet again. If an error happens to be made with respect to the amount of the effect produced, it should be on the side of leniency, rather than on that of severity; for the operation can be always repeated, and more time given on the next occasion, without running any risk of unduly cowing the animal. Whatever punishment we employ, should never be pushed beyond the point necessary to gain our required object, which, in this case, is the attainment of authority over the horse.

My own practice is, with animals that are

Fig. 39.—Horse with his head pulled round when thrown.

simply impatient of control, to produce the desired effect by making them lie down several times; and, with stubborn ones, by keeping them down, with their heads pulled round. The latter method might alone be employed, if the ground be hard or slippery, or if the horse's fore-legs be liable to become sprained. In such cases, both the strait-jacket and throwing gear might be put on the horse, who might be made to lie down with the former, and have his head pulled round by the latter; after doing which, the strait-jacket could be taken off, so as to give the animal entire liberty to kick as much as he pleased. We might use a body-piece on the horse to save the point of his hip that is on the ground, from getting rubbed.

I cannot impress my readers too much with the value, for overcoming stubbornness, of the foregoing method, which, I believe, I have been the first to use.

This throwing gear is exactly similar in its

action to that described in Pratt's book, although differing from it in its construction. Pratt used to employ a rope which was looped round the neck and passed through the mouth, for pulling round the head. He also had a single rope to form both surcingle and crupper. The chief objection to Pratt's method, as far as I can see, was, that the ropes passing through the mouth and under the tail were apt to hurt those parts.

The employment of the tail-rope is an improvement which I have devised, and which I have found most useful. As the surcingle has to be girthed up tight, I like to use a felt saddle-cloth, or numdah, under it, to prevent it slipping forward; in which case, it might squeeze the withers, or the crupper might rub the root of the tail.

In order to make a horse "give in" to the required degree, after he submits to lie down readily with one leg tied up, I like to continue the process with both fore-legs free, until he goes down without any trouble.

Fig. 40.—Best method of keeping a horse on the ground that has fallen in harness.

The process of obtaining control over the horse, as a rule, had best be completed in one lesson, which can be repeated as may be required.

We may utilise the knowledge that a horse cannot get up off the ground, when his head is pulled round, for keeping him down—for instance, when he has fallen in harness—by holding his head in an upward and backward direction, while keeping his neck bent by aid of the pressure of the knee (see Fig. 40).

CHAPTER V.

GIVING HORSES GOOD MOUTHS.

Mouthing gear—Bridling and saddling a horse for the first time—Mouthing on foot.

Mouthing gear.—The gear I use for giving a horse a good mouth—in other words, for teaching him to obey the indications of the rein and leg—consists of a bridle with a heavy, smooth snaffle, which has leather guards on each side; a standing martingale; long reins; a driving pad, or cross-trees which prevent the reins going over the horse's back, and which is kept in place by a crupper and rein-bearers hanging down on each side of the quarters (see Figs. 41 and 42).

The standing martingale is attached to the

Fig. 41.—Horse with driving gear on.

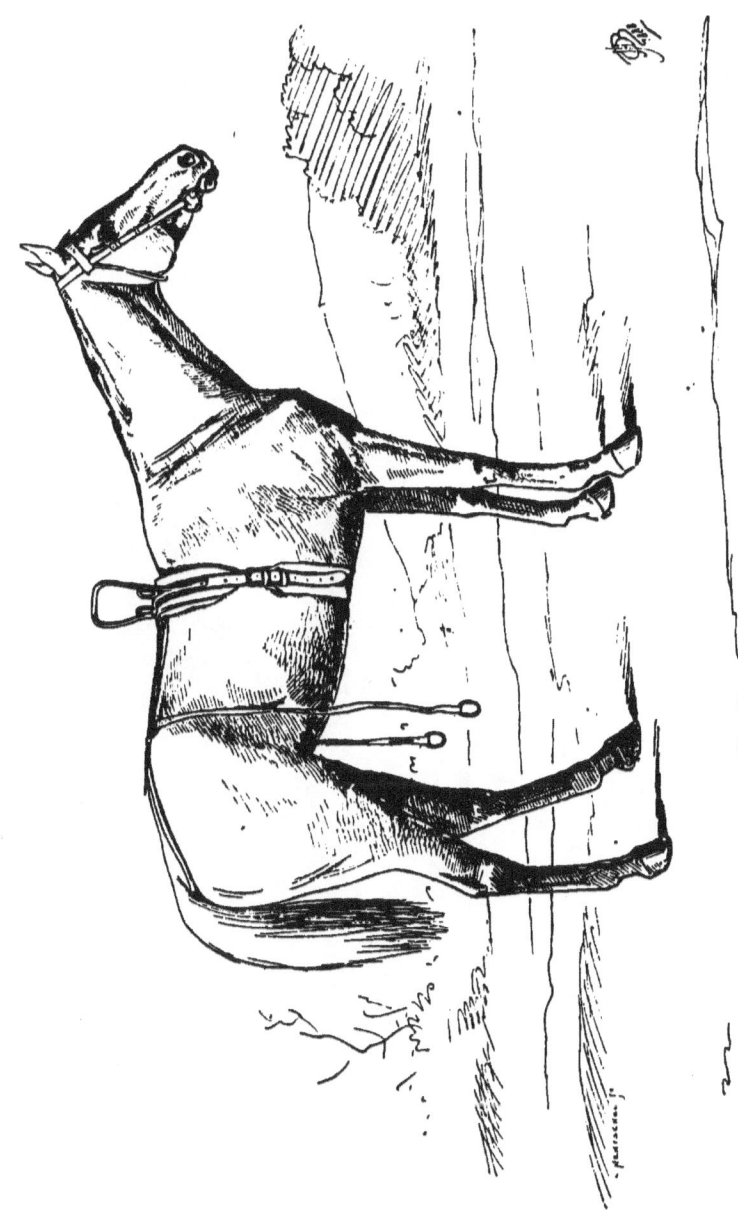

Fig. 42.—Horse with driving pad on, new model.

rings of the snaffle and to the girth of the driving pad, and is lengthened out, as much as is compatible with its preventing the animal from getting the snaffle off the bars of his lower jaw, and on to the corners of his mouth (see page 70 and Fig. 3). The reins are 22 ft. long, are made of 1½ inch "circular" webbing; they pass through the rein-bearers, and buckle on to the rings of the snaffle. The reins are separate from each other; so that, if the horse tries to bolt away when being driven on foot, he can always be pulled round and held fast, by letting go one rein and holding the other tight. The rein-bearers are made about 3 ft. 6 in. long on each side for a horse about 15·2 high, and can be taken up or let out as may be necessary.

Bridling and saddling a Horse for the first time.—These operations may be accomplished with great ease, by means of the rope-twitch (see page 113), and, if necessary, by tying up one fore-leg; especially, if the animal has been rendered quiet in the manner described in Chapter III.

Mouthing on foot.—After making the horse sufficiently steady to pay attention to the instruction about to be given—if this has not already been done—the breaker, while remaining on foot, should take the reins in his hands, and, by gently "feeling the mouth," "clucking" to him, and, at times, cracking the whip, should get him to circle round him, to the left, for instance. If the animal resents the outward rein touching his quarters, the driver should, at first, work with this rein on the driving pad or cross-trees, as in Fig. 41, and then, as the horse gradually learns to bear the pressure without flinching, he should bring it down, as in Fig. 44. By the aid of the rope-twitch (see page 113), to be used by an assistant as may be necessary, it is very easy to overcome any resentment the horse may evince to the rein coming against his hind-legs. We need not, except, perhaps, in very rare cases, employ this form of punishment here; for the horse, on finding that the rein does not hurt him, will quickly cease from manifesting irritation at its presence. The employment of pressure with the outward rein will teach the horse the use of support from the rider's outward leg.

When we have got the animal to circle quietly to the left for a few times, we should turn him to the right with the right rein, acting on his mouth and quarters, so as to teach him, on feeling the indication of the rein on his mouth and side, to turn his quarters, as well as his head and neck (see page 56). He should now be circled to the right on the same principle. After he has learned to do his circles readily and collectedly, with the reins hanging down, he should be made to perform them with the outward rein on the driving pad; so as to accustom him to the feel of the rein in the position it would occupy, when he is being ridden, or driven in harness. If he refuses to turn when the rein is on the pad, a cut or two with the whip will soon teach him to come round quickly. When he is perfect in circling and turning at the trot, we should teach him to rein back, taking care to ease the reins and allow him to "collect" himself, after each step he takes to the rear. When turning, stopping, restraining, or reining back the horse, our pull on the reins—to use Mr. John Hubert Moore's expression—should resemble that which we would employ in drawing a cork out of a bottle, it being free from any snatch or jerk. While circling the horse, the breaker should stand to the side and a little to the rear of the animal (see Fig. 43). This mouthing on foot should, I think, be confined almost entirely to circling, with, of course, frequent changes, and occasional reining back, and should be continued until the required softness of mouth and suppleness of neck are attained. If the animal be found to be "harder" on one side of the mouth, than on the other, he should be worked more on the former, than on the latter;

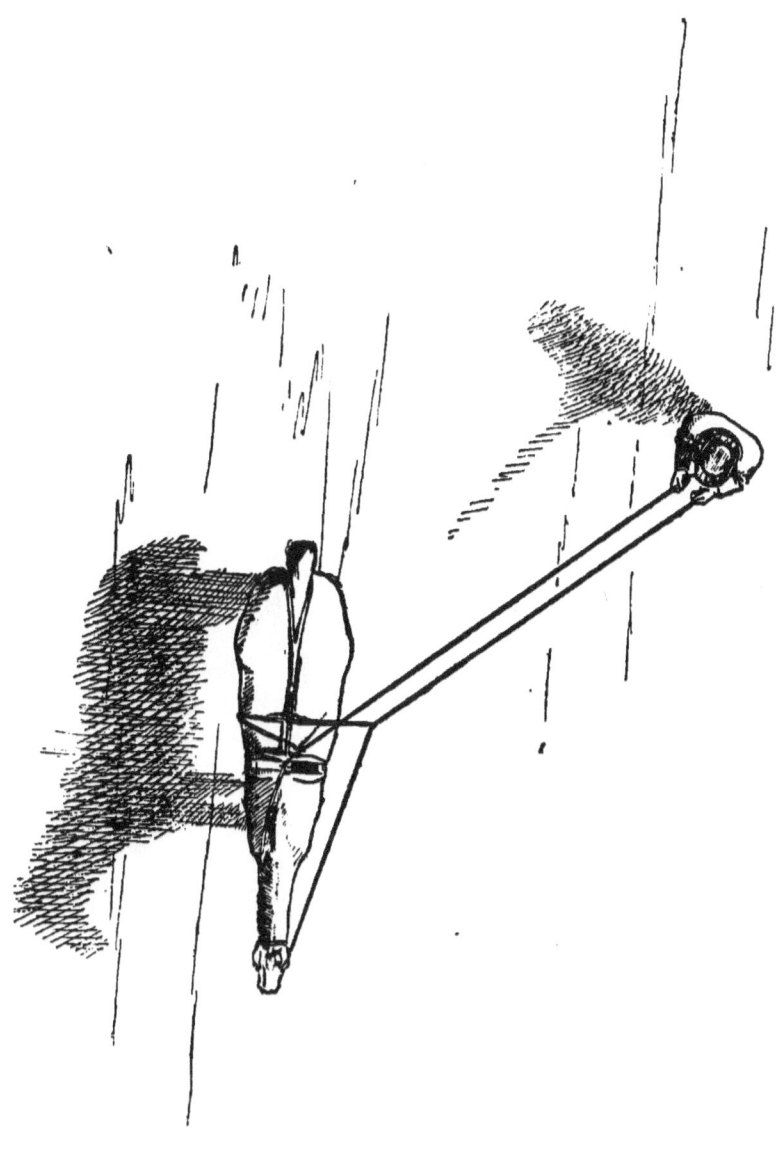

until he goes equally well on both. The reader need only see this method of driving on foot practically demonstrated, to recognise its immense utility, and to acknowledge the fact that it entirely does away with any necessity for the objectionable process of lunging (see page 64).

American horse-tamers use the long reins, without the standing martingale or driving pad, and pass them through rings on a specially prepared surcingle, through the shaft tugs of ordinary single harness, or through the irons of stirrup leathers. Men who try to mouth horses in this manner, are apt to fail to teach their pupils to bend their necks to the rein, and, at the same time, to go up to the bridle; for the animal thus instructed, will always be liable to resist the action of the mouth-piece by chucking up his head and getting the mouth-piece off the bars, and on to the corners of the mouth. In breaking for harness, and, especially, for fast trotting on level ground, the necessity for teaching the horse to bend his neck, to get his hind-quarters under him, and to moderate his speed in response to a pull on the reins, is not nearly so imperative, as in educating the charger, hunter and steeple-chaser, who must have always a "spare leg," ready for any emergency.

The principle of the specially constructed driving pad and cross-trees, is an idea of my own, which I have found of great use. By its employment, we have no need of the bearing reins, which some of the old Irish breakers were accustomed to use; for, if the horse holds his head too low down, it can be easily got up into its proper position when circling the animal, by "playing" with the outward rein, which, in this case, should rest on the driving pad. I cannot approve of rendering the neck rigid by the combined employment of martingale and bearing reins. With respect to the objections to the use of the last-mentioned appliance, see page 55. With skittish animals that jump about much when being mouthed, and with horses that rear, the standing martingale is of great service in preventing the rein getting over the back, and in giving the breaker command over these refractory subjects. Besides this, I find that the presence of the driving pad and rein-bearers is of great use in allowing me to shift the rein up and down as I like.

The breaker should avoid driving the horse on foot, straight in front of him, more than he can help; for, if he does so, he can hardly escape, at times, from keeping a "dead pull" on the animal's mouth. The objectionable practice of driving "youngsters" on foot for miles along a road, as may be seen in full operation at Newmarket and other training resorts, is the fruitful cause of the dead mouths and habit of boring possessed by many race-horses. The young animal, to relieve the bars of his mouth of the constant pressure of the mouth-piece, naturally, gets his chin into his chest, in order to transfer a portion of the pull on to the crown of his head. Instead of acting in this fashion, the breaker, if he wants to take his pupil for a walk on foot, might, after having mouthed him in the manner I have described, put on the leading-rein crupper (see page 148), and lead him where he wished, without incurring any risk of spoiling his mouth.

The whole of this mouthing on foot, might be taught the horse in one lesson of, say, an hour's duration. With a young animal that had never been bridled before, the instruction might be spread over two days, a couple of lessons of half-an-hour's duration each, being given on each day. In point of fact, one or two lessons will, in almost all cases, be sufficient to teach the horse to obey the indications of the rein properly. After that, he will require only a few days' careful riding and bending to make his mouth perfect.

If the animal prove headstrong or sulky, he

should be brought under control, in the manner described in the preceding chapter.

The method of mouthing which I have described, is as applicable to "spoiled" horses, as it is to animals that have never been handled. To my thinking, one great beauty in it—apart from its immense advantage of never giving the animal the chance of getting the upper hand, which he might easily do, were the rider in the saddle—is, that the breaker who employs it, can tell at any moment how his pupil is progressing, by his touch on the reins, and can, accordingly, with well-grounded confidence, use his own judgment in regulating the amount of instruction. The man, however, who trusts to tying the horse up with side- or pillar-reins to the breaking snaffle, in order to get his mouth soft, must necessarily work, more or less, in the dark, and by rule of thumb. Instead of tying a horse up in a fixed position, and thereby cramping the action of his muscles, we retain them supple and ready to respond to our slightest touch, by keeping them in a constant state of change, from contraction to relaxation, without, however, inducing fatigue, the effect of which, on the nerves, is to cause the muscles to work in a slow and ill-regulated manner.

After having broken the horse thoroughly to the snaffle, we may, if required for special work, break him, in the same manner, to the curb, the principles of which I have described in my book on *Riding on the Flat and Across Country*.

When one is unprovided with a driving pad made after my pattern, one may use, as a makeshift, a saddle, through the stirrup-irons of which one may pass the reins (see Fig. 44); not forgetting the standing martingale, a substitute for which may be readily made by connecting the rings of the snaffle to the rings of a running martingale, by a loop of leather, or cord.

Colonel Wardrop, who commands the 12th Lancers, shewed me a method he practises, of driving horses over jumps with long ropes which pass

Fig. 44.—Driving on foot.

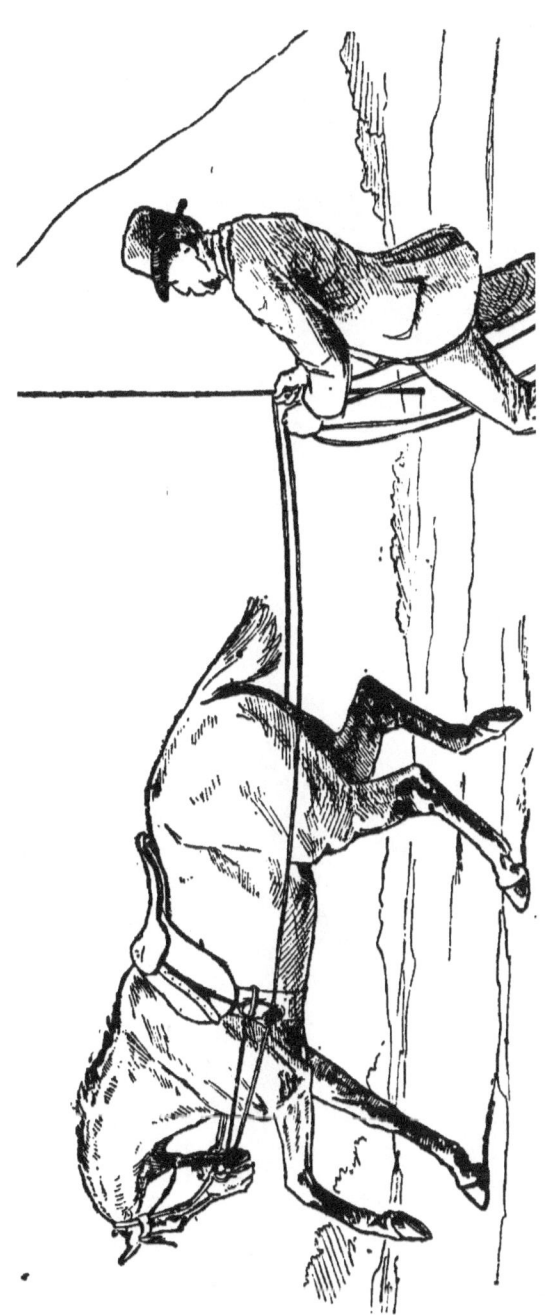

through the stirrup-irons and rings of the snaffle, and are fixed on tightly to the girths and stirrup-irons, on their respective sides (see Fig. 45). This excellent authority on the art of training horses to safely negotiate the difficult lines of country met with in Ireland, tells me that he has found this method of great use for teaching horses to "gather themselves together" in proper style, when coming up to the big banks and ditches that may be seen to perfection in the counties of Kildare and Tipperary. For reasons which I have fully explained in this book, I would advise that the horse should, at first, be thoroughly taught to obey the indications of the rein in the manner I have described. After that, Colonel Wardrop's plan might be useful for giving the horse a few practical lessons over the obstacles in question.

CHAPTER VI.

TEACHING HORSES TO JUMP.

BEFORE this instruction is commenced, the horse ought to be got under control, and thoroughly well mouthed. We may begin to teach him to jump in an enclosure, similar to that described on page 77 : first of all, making him circle and turn with the long reins on foot, at a smart trot. A rounded log of wood, not less than 15 feet in length, and 10 inches or more in diameter, may then be placed across the horse's track, which should have been made soft. If the animal shews a little reluctance to face the obstacle, we may "work" him up to it with the reins, keeping him straight by the pressure of the outward rein against his quarter, as he turns from one side to the other, and stimulating him with the voice and sound of the whip. If he persists in refusing, we should put on the crupper leading-rein (see page 148), and after running him about, and pulling him from side to side by it, a few times, in order to make him understand its use, we should try to lead him over in this manner. Or, having given it to an assistant to go on in front, we may give him another trial with the long reins. In this, as in all other breaking operations with the horse, we should exercise great patience, and should renew our efforts again and again if we do not at first succeed. If the animal "shews fight," I would advise that the whip should be put aside altogether; for the moment, according to my experience, its cut, or even crack, fails to prompt him to go on, it will incite him to offer increased resistance. Instead of its effect, we should employ that of the long reins, in circling him, turning him sharply and backing him, until he gives in, or until we are forced to employ stronger means. Mr. John Hubert Moore, who taught me this admirable method for curing this and other forms of jibbing, considers that its great efficacy is due to the punishment inflicted on the animal's mouth and hocks. Professor Sample, however, holds that it is owing to the fact of the animal imagining that he has no power to resist the command to go forward, after having been forced to turn as the breaker wished. I may observe that it is not the act of turning a jibber to the right and to the left which will overcome his sulkiness, but its continued repetition; and that the sharper this is done the better will be the effect. Hence, I am inclined to think that the punishment theory is the right one. The horse seems, as with the rope-twitch (see page 111), to fail to connect the idea of pain, in this case, with the man who inflicts it, as he undoubtedly does, when whipped, or spurred; and, probably, on that account, yields the more readily to its influence.

If the animal prove thoroughly stubborn, and time be of consequence, he should be made to lie down, and held with his head turned round (see page 158), until he appears to "give in." The driving gear should be again put on, and another trial given. This process may have to be repeated. Such strong measures will hardly ever be necessary, if we commence with the fence low enough.

When putting the animal through the course of the discipline which I have described, for overcoming stubbornness by the use of the long reins, I have found that the good effect has been greatly increased, by utilising the action of the outward rein on the pad.

The log may be gradually raised to a height of three feet, which will be sufficient for the first lesson, and the horse made to jump freely, when circling to the right, as well as to the left. A second fence may be made on the other side of the enclosure, opposite to the first one. When the horse has learned to jump with the outward rein low down, he should be taught to do so with it resting on the pad; as it will then be, more or less, in the position it will occupy, when held by the rider.

By teaching a horse in an enclosure, he will be free from outside disturbing influences, and, having become accustomed to go round the track, will the more readily jump any obstacle placed across it.

By this method, horses may quickly learn to jump, and not alone to clear the obstacle, but also to negotiate it in the exact style they are required to do, when a man is on their back. The more horses are practised in this manner, the more they appear to like jumping, and very rarely exhibit, as they will do with a rider, any dislike to the work, from numerous repetitions, backwards and forwards, over the same fence.

The old plan of teaching a horse to jump by leading him over fences with a cavesson and one or two leading-reins, is an abomination that no horseman should perpetrate; for its tendency is to make the animal jump in the very way he ought not to do, namely, with the weight on the fore-hand, and not on the hind-quarters. Besides this, horses are very apt to resist any forward pull on either cavesson or head-stall. The action of the crupper leading-rein, on the contrary, while leaving the head entirely free, is to make the horse get his hind-legs well under him, as we may see by the way he throws up his hind-quarters, when being led by it over a fence. We all have, of course, heard the well-founded objection to the use of the cavesson and leading-rein for teaching horses to jump, that it makes them slow to "get away" on landing over a fence; a fault, no doubt, caused by the habit of having the weight on the fore-hand. If we want a horse to jump "big" and "get away" quick, we must "catch a good hold of his head;" the very opposite of which is done by the cavesson method.

o

The system of turning horses loose into a small circular course, fenced in and provided with obstacles, and then making them jump with a long whip, is good as far as it goes; but neither it, nor the lunging plan, has any pretensions to teaching obedience to the rein when jumping, without which a safe and clever style is unattainable.

By using a circular track, the horse can be taught to jump at any pace, and the nature of the fences, which should never be made weak enough to "chance," varied as may be desired. The breaker might have three circles, each containing three jumps of different kinds; for instance, a post and rails, water jump, hurdle, double bank, stone wall, hedge, open ditch, ditch and bank, and bank and ditch.

Two or three lessons of this sort will be sufficient to make the generality of horses clever enough to carry a rider in good style. The horse should then be saddled; a man or boy put up, without giving him, at first, any reins to hold; and the horse driven over the fences, as before. When the breaker finds that the animal jumps as well with the man up as he did without him, he may take off the long reins, put on the ordinary ones, and hand them to the rider, who should then take the horse over the fences as before; the breaker using the crack of the whip, as a stimulus, if required. The rider should not be given spurs, unless he is a fine horseman, and unless the horse requires them to make him more lively; but not as a means for overcoming any reluctance he may have to jumping, which should be accomplished in the manner I have laid down.

After the animal has learned all we can teach him in our enclosures, he should be made over to a good rider, to school him in the country, and, if possible, with hounds.

I need hardly say, that a horse should not be jumped, if he is at all sore on his legs or feet.

This plan of schooling horses over a circular

line of fences, was, in my case, the natural outcome of the practice I adopted during my various tours, of breaking horses in a square enclosure of about 20 yards side. I have never seen or heard of it done by any one else, except those I have taught; although it could hardly fail to suggest itself to a person accustomed to drive horses on foot, in a confined space, with the object of teaching them to jump.

One great advantage, among many others, of teaching a horse to jump in the way I have detailed, is, that, by circling and turning the animal in front of the fences, we can cure him of all impetuosity caused by their proximity, and, at the same time, make him willing to jump, with thorough light-heartedness, the moment he receives the indication from the rein to go straight, and clear the obstacle. We can all understand, how valuable such training is, for the hunter and trooper.

CHAPTER VII.

MOUNTING HORSES FOR THE FIRST TIME.

HAVING rendered the horse quiet, given him a good mouth, and taught him to jump, we may next proceed to mount him in the following safe and easy manner, which, I believe, I have been the first to adopt. Put on a snaffle bridle, and knot the reins on the animal's neck, so that they will not hang down. Place over the bridle a head-stall, to the off-side D of which, attach a short leading-rein, and saddle the horse. Take a strong cord; tie a double sheet bend in the hair of the tail with one end of it (see Fig. 30); pass the other end through the D of the halter on the near side; pull the horse's head well round, and secure the cord by a slip knot. If the animal resents his head being brought round, tie him loosely at first, and let him go round and round, stopping him, if necessary, by catching hold of the leading-rein until he stands still. When he does this, he may be tied a little tighter, and so on. The requisite extent to which the head should be turned round, will be attained when he is tied up just short of what would cause him to fall down, if he were allowed to go round on his own account. The outer girth should be unloosed, passed over the cord, and buckled again, so as to bring the cord close to the animal's near side (see Fig. 46); or the surcingle may be placed over it. Having taken the leading-rein in the left hand, we should walk the horse round and round several times, testing him as to his amenability to discipline by stopping him by means of the leading-rein, and then pulling him round again. If he resists these actions on our part, we may feel convinced that he is not under proper control. In which case, we may continue

Fig. 46.—Horse prepared to be mounted for the first time.

Fig. 47.—Second stage in breaking a horse for riding.

to make him revolve, or may force him to lie down, and hold him with his head turned round, as described on page 158, until he gives in.

As many horses, especially Australian buckjumpers, are very shy of being touched with the heels, or even gripped closely with the knees, it is well to try if the animal we have in hand is affected with this form of timidity. For this object, we may gently prod the horse with the rounded end of a pole, in the ribs, while an assistant takes him round with the leading-rein, until he ceases to mind the touch of the pole. A few applications of the rope-twitch (see page 113), will also have a good effect in rendering him quiet in this respect. We may now get an assistant to catch hold of the mane, on the near side, with his left hand, the stirrup-iron with his right hand, and go through the various stages of mounting, beginning with putting his left foot in the stirrup (see Fig. 47), catching the pommel or cantle of the saddle, as he sees fit, with the right hand, and hopping round on the right foot, while we keep the horse revolving by means of the leading-rein. I may add that the Australian rough-riders, who are marvellously expert at getting on to a difficult horse, place the right hand on the pommel of the saddle, and not on the cantle, as is the practice in other places, and consequently place the left hand high up on the mane. As a matter of course, the assistant should not finally throw his leg over, until the animal ceases to resist. When the horse has got accustomed to the presence of the man in the saddle, the rider may touch him with his heels, lightly at first, and gradually stronger, without hurting him, until he stands the contact unmoved. When the horse has stopped trying to get free, we may slacken off the cord a little, take him round and round again, and so on, until it is safe to let him loose altogether. Before doing this, we should, as before, test his quietness, by stopping him with the leading-rein, and then pulling him round again. When most of the tension has been taken off the cord, we may give the leading-rein to the rider, to hold in his right hand, so that he can stop the horse if necessary; while we make the animal go round by touching him lightly with the whip. After the cord has been removed, the rider may take the reins, and keep the animal, at first, going round in small circles, and, then, gradually enlarging them, until he can take the horse in any direction he likes.

In all my experience with numbers of horses that had, for years, successfully resisted the most determined efforts to mount them, I have never failed to accomplish this object in one lesson, by means of the method just described; nor has any horse, after I have removed the cord, shewed the slightest return to unruliness. The method of making the horse, by the use of the rope-twitch (see page 113), steady to mount, which I shall describe in Chapter IX., is specially valuable for this particular purpose; while the head and tail plan, by producing a powerful moral effect, renders the animal not alone easy to mount, but also quiet to ride. As I have pointed out on page 31, we should, in all cases, confirm the habit of obedience by repetition. I may mention that the method of tying a horse "head and tail," with the object of making him quiet, has been in use for many years; though I am unable to say who was its inventor. If practised without my improvements of leading-rein and surcingle, or girth, over the cord, it has the serious faults, that as soon as the horse begins to revolve quickly, the operator has, practically, no further control over him until he stops of his own accord, or tumbles down "all of a heap," and that it is impossible to mount him safely. The man, if expert, and if the horse has no tendency to hit out with his off-fore, might run in and catch him by the head-stall, if he thought that the animal was in danger of falling, on account of going round too fast. The conduct of such confidential horses, I need hardly say, is not the standard by which we should gauge the safety of any method of breaking, which, in order to be generally useful, should not demand from the person who practises it, the possession of exceptional activity, or foolhardiness. When the off-side leading-rein is on, the breaker can, with perfect safety, catch it while the horse is turning round; for, at that time, it swings entirely clear of the fore-limb, and in a convenient position for the breaker to lay hold of it. If a man mounts a horse tied head and tail, with the cord unconfined by girth or surcingle, he is placed in the uncomfortable dilemma of riding without any "grip" on the saddle, by having his left leg pulled upwards and outwards by the cord, or of having this limb imprisoned between the cord and the animal's side; while, in either case, the man is in a most dangerous position, on an animal that is revolving round and round, with little or no control over its own movements. We may see, therefore, that the simple head and tail method, without the improvements I have described, is not applicable for mounting purposes.

The plan of gaining command over a horse by tying him head and tail, and allowing or forcing him to revolve round until he falls down, is unworthy the consideration of educated men. It is based on the wrong assumption that all ailments of temper spring from the same cause; the supposed remedy is not under the control of the operator; the effect is physical, rather than moral, and consequently is not lasting; and the results of the violent twisting of the hocks, and of the fall, if the animal comes down on the side to which his head is turned, as he often does, are apt to injure him.

Professor Sample gives a thoroughly sound and rational exposition of the head and tail method, which would well repay the attention of all horsemen who have not already seen it. This American gentleman is unrivalled in the marvellous power he possesses of teaching, in a wonderfully short time, horses to perform difficult feats of obedience.

CHAPTER VIII.

BREAKING HORSES FOR LADIES' RIDING.

ALMOST any horse that is quiet for a man to ride, will carry a lady steadily the first time the attempt is made. The few special requirements to make a well-broken-in saddle horse perfect as a lady's hack, are : (1) That he must stand without moving when she is being put on, or when she mounts from a chair or block. (2) That he must not shy at the habit, or sidle away from it. (3) That he must "bend" himself more readily, and go more "collectedly," than if he had to carry a man. (4) That he must understand the touch of the whip on his off side, as equivalent to the pressure of the right leg.

(5) And that he must learn, always, to "strike off," in the canter, with the off fore leading. On a good mover, a fine horsewoman will neither feel, nor exhibit discomfort when the animal may happen to lead with the near fore; although, at first starting, the lead with the other leg is more agreeable. I may add, that the canter is a pace of three time; the succession of beats being: *a*. leading fore; *b*. non-leading fore and its opposite hind-leg; *c*. hind-leg of side opposite to leading fore. Hence, the more a fore-leg leads in the canter, the more likely is it to suffer from the injurious effects of concussion. It is obvious that if we wish to keep a horse sound, we should not let him canter too much with the same leg leading.

The first three of the conditions, just mentioned, which are indispensable to the lady's horse, can be quickly fulfilled by instruction on foot; although the remainder of the animal's education should be completed by a good rider. I may remark, that many ladies ride so well, that any special preparation for their use, is almost needless. Besides this, the short habits of the present day are but little apt to make animals go unsteadily.

The employment of the rope-twitch (see page 113) will speedily correct any unsteadiness at mounting which cannot be remedied, without delay, by ordinary means. The horse may be broken of any tendency to shy at, or sidle away from, the habit, by putting the side-saddle on, fixing a rug to its near side, and giving the animal a few circling lessons on foot with the long reins (see page 172). The same practice, with frequent spells at reining back, will teach him to bend and collect himself to the required extent. Some work with the long reins, while the lady is in the saddle, will do the horse good, if he be at all awkward.

CHAPTER IX.

BREAKING HORSES TO HARNESS.

THE place which I prefer to all others, for breaking a horse to harness, is an enclosure about thirty yards square, the ground of which is level, and hard enough to allow the wheels to run smoothly.

Whether intended partially for saddle purposes, or not, I would advise that the horse should be broken in the manner already described, before trying him between the shafts. Before putting him in, we should circle him for half-an-hour or more, with the long reins on foot (see page 172), and get an assistant, while the animal is going round, to gentle him under the belly and about the hind-quarters, as recommended by Pratt and others, with a long pole, without hurting him, so as to accustom him to its touch. The whip should also be cracked about the horse, without hitting him, until he ceases to mind its noise. If the horse resents these operations, which inflict no pain on him, the rope-twitch (see page 113) may be employed to enforce the required obedience; or the animal may be made to lie down (see page 153), and gentled. When the horse has been made quiet, he will readily take to double harness if put alongside a steady breakhorse for a few times, and, when accustomed to this work, will, as a rule, go by himself without any trouble; although he may be a little awkward at first. If we want to put the animal into single harness, right off, and if we have got the gear at hand, we may harness the horse, put the strait-jacket over the harness, buckling it up, just tight enough, to prevent him kicking when it is on; and then drive him, on foot, with the long reins passed through the shaft-tugs, for a short time. We may now put him into the shafts of some suitable, light two-wheeled trap, retaining the strait-jacket over the harness. Two assistants, one on each side, may be employed to hold separate reins attached to the snaffle, while the driver stands on the near side, on about a line with the wheels, holding another pair of reins, which pass through the rings of the pad, and are, of course, fixed to the snaffle. If sufficient help be at hand, it is an advantage to have two other assistants to hold the traces of the strait-jacket ready to let out or draw tight, as may be required. After the horse has gone quietly for a bit, the strait-jacket may be removed, a kicking-strap substituted, and, after a little, an assistant may be put on the driving seat, with all proper precaution. When the horse has thoroughly settled down to his work, the breaker may get on to the seat, and dispense with the help of the other men, if he sees fit. With one man to hold the rope-twitch, and with the aid of a kicking-strap, the breaker, if expert, may easily manage to put a horse in single harness for the first time. In an enclosure such as I have described, the breaker may circle the horse in the trap, with the long reins on foot, by himself, and, in a short time, after the animal has settled down, he may get an assistant to sit in the trap. When the horse is found to go quietly inside the enclosure, he may be tried outside. I think it always the best and easiest plan to break a horse to harness, without blinkers.

CHAPTER X.

FAULTS OF MOUTH.

Boring—Chucking up the head—Pulling—Rearing—Shying—Stargazing—Tender-mouthed—Turn, difficult to—Yawing.

THE classification of vices and faults adopted in this, and the following chapters, is, necessarily, somewhat arbitrary; as their causes are more often complex, than simple. The fact of many of them not possessing generally accepted names, has obliged me, in some cases, to sacrifice elegance and correctness of expression, for an attempt at conciseness and clearness of meaning.

Boring.—When the horse has got into the habit of carrying his head too low, we should get it into proper position by circling the animal on foot with the long reins (see page 172), and by reining him back. When he bores on one rein more than the other, we should adopt the same procedure ; although we should devote our attention, mainly, to getting him to turn readily to the side on which his mouth is "hard," until he bends to it, as easily as to the other. After half-an-hour's judicious driving, the horse ought to carry himself, and obey the rein in the desired manner; although he may require half-a-dozen lessons to confirm the habit.

Chucking up the head.—Here we should teach the horse, in the manner just described, to "save" his mouth, by carrying his head in a proper position, and by bending his neck to the pull of the rein (see remarks on the standing martingale, page 70). Mr. Kemp, A.V.D., tells me that the animal may be easily broken of this objectionable habit by using a nose-band, inside the part that goes over the nose, three or four cowrie shells [small marbles would have the same effect] are sewn; the nose-band being kept in position by a standing martingale, which, of course, should be of the proper length (see page 70). This plan is on the same principle, as the method I have described; for, in both, the horse relinquishes the trick, on finding out that its practice inflicts pain, and that he can save himself from punishment, by obeying the rein.

Pulling.—We should give the hard puller, at least, a dozen lessons with the long reins on foot, teaching him, somewhat sharply, that he must obey the rein. It is, also, well to use the word "whoa," or any other suitable one, as recommended by Pratt, Magner, and others, whenever we pull him up; so that he may learn to stop on hearing it. Making him lie down and keeping him on the ground (see page 158) will be of great service in reducing the runaway to obedience.

The breaker will naturally have to regulate the severity and frequency of this beneficial discipline, as he may see fit.

Rearing.—The rearer should, in the same manner, be taught to swing his quarters round, on either rein being pulled, with the outward rein kept low down; and, when he is perfect at this, the lesson should be completed, with this rein on the driving pad. If he rears, as a defence against the action of the rein, the breaker should pull all the harder. If this brings the animal " over ; " so much stronger will be the effect produced. When jibbing is combined with rearing, if we find that the desired result is not obtained by the process of driving on foot, as speedily as we may wish; we may make the horse lie down, and keep him on the ground, with his head turned round (see page 158), until he gives in. We may also apply the same discipline to those terribly dangerous animals that endeavour to crush their rider, by throwing themselves backward.

Shying.—Leaving out all cases of shying which are due to defective sight, I venture to say that the vast majority of shyers can be made to relinquish this annoying trick, merely by giving them good mouths with the long reins on foot. This mouthing practice, not alone, makes the horse attentive, as well as obedient, to the indications of the rein, but it also teaches discipline, and gives the animal confidence in his director; and, hence, removes the two causes of shying: namely, fear, and wilfulness. If the shyer shows great timidity, which is often combined with impatience of control (see page 4), the animal should be rendered quiet, as described in Chapter III. All these remarks apply equally well to shying off the ball at polo, and off the peg at tent-pegging, and to other forms of yawing about, and not going straight.

Stargazing.—See "Chucking up the head."

Tender-mouthed.—We may overcome any undue

tenderness of the mouth, or unwillingness to "go up to the bridle," by circling the horse on foot with the long reins, with, and without, a rider on the animal's back. When the horse finds that he does not get his mouth "pulled about," he will, in two or three lessons, gain confidence, and will allow a steady pull on the reins.

Turn, difficult to.—The practice with the long reins on foot, advocated for the correction of shying, etc., will be found to be an effective remedy in this case; and is specially applicable for polo ponies that shy off the ball, and are difficult to turn quickly.

"*Yawing.*"—The animal may be broken of this habit, when ridden, of going from side to side, instead of straight, by the method recommended for shying.

CHAPTER XI.

NERVOUSNESS AND IMPATIENCE OF CONTROL.

Buck-jumping—Difficult to bridle, handle, mount, dismount, ball, or drench—Difficult to put into a railway train, ship's horse-box, etc.—Difficult to shoe—Nervous of being touched with the heel—Unsteady with the whip; under fire; when drawing swords, etc.

Buck-jumping.—The best procedure I know to overcome this vice, is to circle the horse with the long reins on foot, frequently turning him (see "Shying," page 220), for about half-an-hour; make him lie down, and keep him on the ground with his head turned round (see page 158), till he, apparently, "gives in"; then let him up; tie him head and tail, and saddle him, with one girth over the cord (see page 197); let him revolve round, and while he does so, gentle him on the ribs with the end of the long pole (see page 203), until he stands its touch. The horse can now be mounted in the manner described on page 197. If we have got a rider that does not mind the chance of a fall, we may omit the head and tail business, and have the horse saddled and mounted with the long reins on him, when he recovers his feet after undergoing his discipline on the ground. The breaker who holds the long reins, should pull the horse round, from side to side, the moment the assistant gets into the saddle; and, having obtained control over him, should circle and turn him several times, until he goes quite freely. The long reins can now be taken off, and the snaffle reins given to the rider, who, previous to this, should not touch the reins; although he may use the breast-plate, or other convenient object, as an aid, in case of accident, for retaining his balance.

Difficult to bridle, handle, mount, dismount, ball, or drench.—Teaching the animal, with the rope-twitch, to pay attention to the word "steady!" (see page 111), will cure all these vices. In Chapter III. I have described at some length various methods to be adopted with horses difficult to handle. The use of the rope-twitch is singularly efficacious for making animals steady to mount and dismount. Mr. D. C. Pallin, A.V.D., informs me that he has invariably succeeded with horses that were deemed impossible to drench, in making them drink, by mounting them; sitting well forward; drawing the head round to the off-side by the head-stall with the left hand; and then giving them the draught out of a bottle with the right hand. This gentleman also advises to have a man on the back of a horse that is difficult to ball, while the operator is giving the bolus. I need hardly say that the aim of these expedients, valuable as they are, is to make the horse take the drench, or ball, at the time, and not to make him permanently quiet, in this respect.

Difficult to put into a railway train, ship's horse-box, etc.—Use the crupper leading-rein, the rope-twitch, or the Comanche bridle (see page 261), or both. Before making the actual attempt, the appliance, whichever one be used, should be put into requisition a few times, so that the animal may understand what is demanded of him.

Difficult to shoe.—Use the rope-twitch (see page 113); lift the foot, if a fore one, with the rope-noose (see page 88), or suspend it from the surcingle (see page 102); if a hind one, with the hobble, and double cord attached to the tail (see page 135). Gentle the limb, and gradually accustom the hoof to the hammer; correcting the horse with the twitch, if obliged to do so. If the horse be very obstinate, or very violent, it may be well to bring him under control, by making him lie down, and, if necessary, holding him down with his head pulled round (see page 158).

Nervous of being touched with the heel.—Tie the horse head and tail and gentle him with the end of the long pole in the ribs (see page 203); or use the rope-twitch while the rider is in the saddle, and while he touches the animal, so as not to hurt him, with his unarmed heel.

Unsteady with the whip; under fire; when drawing swords, etc.—Teach the horse, while he is under the provocation to which he objects, by the use of the rope-twitch (see page 113), to stand quietly on receiving the command "steady!"; or use the head-and-tail method.

CHAPTER XII.

JIBBING IN SADDLE.

SPEAKING generally, we may consider jibbing to be the determined manifestation of stubbornness in the horse.

Acting on the sound principle that we should apply no more coercion to the animal than is absolutely necessary, we should at first try the effect of driving the jibber, on foot, with the long reins (see page 172). After it has consented to go quietly without anyone on its back, we may put an assistant in the saddle without giving him the reins, and continue driving the animal until it moves freely in every direction. The rider may then take the reins, and circle and turn the animal several times before taking it for a regular ride. If the horse resolutely sulks, the breaker, to expedite matters, may make it lie down with the proper tackle and hold it down, with its head turned round (see page 158), until it, apparently, gives in; after which it may get another trial at circling. If it still resists, it should be put down again, and, so on, for three, or four times. This change of discipline is most efficacious for the jibber, who quickly seems to recognise the fact, that the irksome constraint on the ground is a punishment for its misbehaviour. Having failed, after putting forth all its powers of opposition, to resist the one form of coercion, it will have but little energy left to stiffen its neck against the other. By adopting this plan with patience, as well as firmness, and without using the whip, except to crack it, the breaker ought to succeed with almost any jibber in one lesson of a couple of hours' duration. The desired effect can be produced much easier in a secluded enclosure, than in the open. I believe I have been the first to employ this method of making a horse lie down in combination with the driving on foot as a remedy for jibbing.

It is not uncommon to meet with, in the mounted branches of the Army, horses that will go anywhere in company, but will refuse to quit the ranks by themselves, or to act as single riding horses. This peculiarity; the habit of trying to shoulder the rider's leg up against a wall, tree, or other convenient object; and all other forms of jibbing, should be treated in the manner just described.

For jibbing in harness, see page 236.

CHAPTER XIII.

JUMPING FAULTS.

"Chancing" fences—Jumping too slowly—Refusing—Running out at fences—Rushing at fences.

"*Chancing*" *fences.* — This dangerous fault may be corrected by driving the horse with the long reins over fences (see Chapter VI.) which are too stiff to chance, but which are well within the compass of the animal's powers.

Jumping too slowly.—Many horses commit this fault without attempting, in any way, to refuse. It is often caused by the practice of teaching animals to jump by means of the cavesson and leading-rein; for, by employing this method, the weight is unduly thrown on the fore-hand, and consequently the horse, not having his hind-legs well under him when he "lands" over the fence, is unable to get quickly away from it. Besides this, the horse has to moderate his speed in accordance with that of the man in front of him. By driving horses with the long reins on foot, in the manner described in Chapter VI., we teach them to go with their hind-legs well under them and at any pace we like; and, by so doing, we can quickly get them out of the habit of "dwelling" at their fences.

"*Refusing.*" — See Chapters VI. and XII. Before taking in hand a horse that jumps "unkindly," we should carefully examine him in order to see if his fault arises from disease, or infirmity. If such be the case, the animal should not be tried at jumping, until he is sound.

Running out at fences.—For this, we should use

the long reins on foot. By their proper employment, we can make a horse go so straight that he will turn neither to one side, nor to the other, when jumping a 3 ft. 6 in. post and rails, for instance, which is only 3 ft. long, and is unprovided with wings of any sort.

Rushing at fences.—This fault can also be easily overcome by the employment of the long reins on foot, and the horse made to regulate his pace, according to the wish of his rider, without shewing any impatience.

CHAPTER XIV.

VICES IN HARNESS.

Difficult to harness—Difficult to unharness—Getting the tail over the rein and kicking—Hanging against the pole—Jibbing—Kicking—Lying down—Plunging forward at starting—Pulling away from the pole—Undue fear of the whip.

Difficult to harness. — Place the trap in the centre of the enclosure, and drive the horse, on foot, with the long reins, all about it, and back him between the shafts, so that he may get accustomed to it. We may then tie up one foreleg, apply the rope-twitch, and have the horse harnessed by drawing up the cart, while he is kept standing still. After repeating this, once or twice, the leg may be let down, and the harnessing performed as before. After the horse has become quite steady, he may be backed into the shafts.

Or, we may put the strait-jacket on over the harness, make the horse lie down two or three times with it, and having got him on to his feet again, draw the traces of the strait-jacket so tight, that, if he attempt to move, he will fall down. While keeping him in this position, we may try to bring the shafts over his back, letting him fall if he begins to struggle. In the great majority of cases, the horse will quickly learn to regard the falling down as a punishment for his unsteadiness, which he cannot resist; and will accordingly give in, and stand quietly. After he does so, we may gradually slacken out the traces of the strait-jacket, until we can remove this apparatus altogether. We may tie up the leg, or employ the rope-twitch, as may be advisable. For safety sake, in single harness, we should use a kicking-strap. If the animal is very determined in his resistance, we may take the obstinacy out of him, by making him lie down, and keeping his head turned round (see page 158).

Difficult to unharness.—Use the rope-twitch, which will be sufficient in almost all cases. To prevent the animal springing forward, we may employ the strait-jacket, or make him lie down.

Getting the tail over the rein and kicking.—I regret to say that I know no means of permanently breaking a horse of the habit of whisking his tail over the rein, at times, when it is within reach. We may, however, by driving the animal on foot, and accustoming him to bear the rein under the tail, or by using the rope-twitch (see page 113), teach the horse not to kick, when he finds the rein in that position. I presume that the horse might be taught, by the rope-twitch, not to whisk his tail over the rein, on feeling it touch his hind-quarters; although, not having practically tested this expedient, I cannot speak positively as to its merits. I have rendered several animals that were previously addicted to the habit in question, quiet when the rein got under their tails, or touched their quarters, by the means described; and by gentling those parts when the animal was tied head and tail (see page 203). I have met some cases, in which the kicking was caused by pain due to pressure on melanotic tumours that were on the under surface of the dock.

Hanging against the pole.—The remedy, here, would be driving with the long reins. For the first few times that the animal was driven with another horse, he might have a pair of reins to himself, as well as the pair which connects him to his fellow.

Jibbing.—We should break the unharnessed horse of jibbing in the manner described in Chapter XII., and may then put him in a light trap, inside the enclosure, and try to circle him, with the long reins, on the side to which he more readily bends. Having accomplished this, we should endeavour to get him, by a wide sweep, to turn to the other rein, and, if we are successful, should circle him freely in it; turning and changing him, as we may deem advisable. If the animal remain obstinate, we should take him out, and put him again through the necessary discipline of the long reins; or we may keep him on the ground with his head turned round (see Chapter XII.). As soon as we think he has given in, we may put him into the shafts, and give him another trial. In attempting to start, or turn the animal, we should, on no account, use the whip, except, perhaps, to crack it; but should continue to pull the horse's head from side to side with the reins, so as to make him strike off in the desired direction. I think it best to refrain from speaking to the horse, while all this is being done. When the horse circles and turns with perfect obedience to the rein, we may, while keeping him at a walk, get an assistant to quietly mount into the trap, and give him the reins, as soon as the animal shews that he does not mind his presence behind him. The horse may now be taken into the open, and circled and turned by the man in the cart, a few times, before being taken for a steady drive.

Before the animal is harnessed, we should satisfy ourselves that the jibbing is not caused by any ailment, such as sore shoulders, which should be cured before we proceed further.

We should be careful not to use any words, or other signals that might remind the animal of previous acts of disobedience which, presumedly, had been successful in their object. As before remarked, I like to use, when breaking a horse of jibbing, a plain bridle; because I find animals go kinder without blinkers, than with them.

If a jibber appears afraid of the whip, it is well, in the first instance, to prove to him (see page 241) that we are not going to hurt him, when we crack it, or flourish it about.

Kicking.—We should put the animal through

the course of discipline described in Chapter IX. The strait-jacket put on loosely, or the kicking-strap, will prevent him doing any mischief. Before putting the animal between the shafts, he should be well driven with the long reins, for from thirty minutes, to an hour; so that he may pay attention to the indications of the rein. If he persists in kicking, he should be made to lie down, and, then, gentled on the ground; or he may be kept down with his head turned round (see page 158) until he gives in. Mr. Mitchell, A.V.D., who is an excellent breaker, tells me that he has obtained admirable results with bad kickers, by fixing, parallel to their sides, two stout poles, each about 7 feet long, secured in front of the chest and behind the quarters, so that the animal cannot get free from them; and then letting him kick, till he is tired. This method, by giving the horse nothing to kick at, will soon teach him the uselessness of doing so. In most cases, I would be inclined to use the rope-twitch, in order to make the horse learn the salutary lesson of connecting, in his own mind, the idea of punishment, with the practice of his favourite vice.

The old expedient of tying a kicker's tail to the splinter bar, is often successful in breaking the animal of this objectionable habit. In other cases, it serves only to aggravate the vice. The tail may, here, be easily secured by a double sheet bend (see Fig. 30).

Lying down.—The habit of lying down in harness, is, no doubt, in many instances, difficult to cure. To accomplish this end, particular attention should be paid to making the animal obey the indications of the rein, by driving him on foot with the long reins. The trap used to practise him in, should be a very light, two-wheeled one. If he lies down, a sharp slap on his muzzle will generally make him jump up. The lesson, of course, should be given in the enclosure. In extreme cases, he should be put through the discipline detailed for jibbing.

Plunging forward at starting.—Use the rope-twitch (see page 113); or drive the animal, in the enclosure, on foot, with the long reins, while he is in the trap, after having given him a good long mouthing lesson (see page 172), and practise him at circling, turning, starting, and pulling up.

Pulling away from the pole.—See that the coupling chain is not too tight. Treat as for " Hanging against the pole " (page 236).

Undue fear of the whip.—Circle the horse with the long reins on foot (see page 172), and get an assistant to crack the whip all about him, without touching him with it, until he ceases to mind it; or do so, while he is tied head and tail. An application or two of the rope-twitch (see page 113) will expedite matters. The breaker should "make much of" the horse, when the animal stands quietly under the provocation given.

CHAPTER XV.

AGGRESSIVENESS.

Biting—Kicking—Savaging—Striking out in front.

Biting.—Apply the wooden gag (see page 145); tie up one fore-leg, or put on the strait-jacket; and gentle the horse all over, to shew him that he cannot bite, and that, when he vainly attempts to do so, he will hurt his mouth, by the pressure of the gag on his gums. On this account, its action is most salutary, and differs entirely from that of a muzzle, which simply protects the object of the animal's resentment, without either checking the practice of the habit, or punishing him for indulging in it. I need hardly say, that, with the gag on, the horse is unable to bring his teeth together. The fore-leg may be let down, or the strait-jacket taken off, as soon as the horse is quiet to handle with the gag alone. This instrument may be kept in the horse's mouth, for an hour at a time, during which period he should be handled with gentleness and freedom; particular care being taken not to irritate the animal, whose confidence and affection we should now endeavour to win. The worst biter ought to be rendered safe to handle, when the gag is out of his mouth, by three of these lessons a day, for two or three days. For safety-sake, the breaker might teach the horse the use of the word "steady!" with the rope-twitch (see page 113). Though many bad, treacherous biters have passed through my hands, I have never met one that would attempt to bite when the gag was taken out of his mouth, after he had been gentled, with it on, for a quarter of an hour, or even less. It might be advisable, with very vicious horses, to make them lie down, and hold them with their heads turned round, until they had "given in" (see page 158).

Kicking.—A horse that tries to deliberately kick anyone that comes within reach, may be broken of the habit by the rope-twitch (see page 113); or by making him lie down (see page 153). In such cases, it is well to thoroughly mouth the animal on foot with the long reins; so as to make him more attentive to the indications of the rein, than to the practice of his favourite vice. The man who drives on foot, in the enclosure, is secure from getting kicked by the horse; for, if the animal attempts to lash out at him, he can always pull the horse's head round with the rein. Mouthing on foot, is specially applicable to horses that are in the habit of kicking at other horses, hounds, etc.

It is advisable to teach a kicker to turn his hind-quarters away from us (see page 86), when we approach him; supposing, of course, that he is free to do so.

Savaging.—Put the animal through the discipline advised for biting, in the preceding paragraph; give several (say, half-a-dozen) good mouthing lessons, with the long reins, on foot; and, if the animal be inclined to savage horses, or men, while being ridden, substitute for the ordinary breaking snaffle, the wooden gag (see page 145) during his mouthing lessons; and, also, ride him in it, for a few times. *Savaging at polo* may be easily cured in this manner.

An expert breaker can always manage to pull round a horse that rushes at him, while the animal is being driven on foot. Even when the horse backs and kicks, as well as attempts to savage, the driver can easily keep him in control, by pulling him round, alternately, with each rein. One has, naturally, to be quicker when a horse rushes at one than when he backs. I confine the expression, "savaging," to the habit some animals have of worrying the object of their dislike, with or without rushing at it; and, "biting," to the simple act of snapping with the teeth. Practical horsemen will understand this somewhat arbitrary distinction. I may remark that horses often bite, without, apparently, any vicious intention.

Striking out in front.—We may tie up one fore-leg, put the strait-jacket on, apply the rope-twitch, or tie the horse head and tail, and then gentle both fore-legs. The use of the rope-twitch will, generally, be found to be the quickest method.

CHAPTER XVI.

RIDING AND DRIVING THE NEWLY-BROKEN HORSE.

HAVING made the horse as perfect as we can on foot, we should complete his education by riding him with skill and judgment. If we find that he shews signs of becoming unruly, or of recommencing some of his old tricks, it is far better to get off, and make him steady, in the manner before detailed, before proceeding further; than to risk any chance of a defeat while on his back. If he happen to develop such symptoms, we may feel assured that the fault is on our side, in having carried out his instruction on foot, in an imperfect manner. As I accord unqualified admiration for our best English and Irish styles of riding, whether on the flat, across country, or in the school, I shall refrain from going over old ground, and shall content myself, here, with adding a few remarks which have special reference to the recently handled animal.

When mounting, the breaker should make the animal stand perfectly still, until it gets the proper indication to move forward.

He should make the horse carry himself in good style, by keeping him up to the bit with the pressure of the leg, and by having a nice light feeling on his mouth.

All horses should be taught to rein back with ease and precision.

According as the animal requires to be bent and collected for his own particular work, so should he be instructed in turning, circling and changing, with the proper leg, shouldering in, and passaging. When the reins are taken up in both hands, they should be used in the same style as that recommended for the long reins (see page 174). If necessary, the horse may now be taught to obey the reins when held in one hand, and may be practised in the use of the curb.

When the horse has learnt to go smoothly, his mouth should be interfered with as little as possible. I am entirely against the practice of keeping the animal in a constant state of attention to signals from the reins; as it makes him rely on his rider, rather than on his own cleverness, to extricate him out of difficulties, and renders him uncertain, and lacking in self-confidence. This is especially the case in jumping, at which work the rider should limit his interference, if the horse is going too fast, to dropping his hands, and taking a pull, thirty or forty yards from the fence, and, then, letting the horse measure his own distance, and take off, as suits him best. If the animal's attention be distracted by the rider's interference at this critical moment, the risk of an accident will be greatly enhanced. The foregoing is the substance of the advice given by Mr. John Hubert Moore to his pupil, that well-known fine horseman, Colonel Hickman of the 21st

Hussars, who attributes the immunity he has enjoyed from bad falls, over all kinds of country, and on all sorts of horses, to its rigid observance.

When the newly-broken horse is put into the shafts, he should be driven according to the principles laid down for riding him, in so far as they apply to harness work.

CHAPTER XVII.

STABLE VICES.

Difficult and vicious to catch—Hanging back on the head-stall—Kicking—Kicking at night—Pawing at night—Pawing back the litter—Rubbing the tail—Sleeping standing.

Difficult and vicious to catch.—If the animal be viciously inclined, make him quiet by the methods described in the preceding chapters. Teach him to come up to you when you call him (see page 261); and to turn his quarters away from you, when you approach him (see page 87).

Hanging back on the head-stall.—The Americans employ the crupper leading-rein (see page 148), to hitch up a horse given to this fault. I have been told that a good way is to shorten the rack chain, by tying it with a piece of thin twine, so that when the animal pulls on the chain, he will break the twine, and will then cease to pull, on the presumed supposition that he has broken the chain. For horses with this habit, it is common to place a broad band across the lower part of the stall, so as to allow the animal to rest against it, if he likes.

Kicking.—See Chapter XV. We may, also, teach the animal to "stand over" in his stall, by pulling his head round with a cord attached to the side of the head-stall, passed through a ring on the top of the roller, and carried outside of the stall, while giving, simultaneously with the pull on the cord, some appropriate verbal order, such as "over!" (See Fig. 47.)

Kicking at night.—I have no experience in breaking horses of this habit. I would suggest the employment of the strait-waistcoat, which should

be loose enough to allow the animal to lie down and get up. I have seen it recommended, in such cases, to hang some soft object, such as a large bag filled with hay, behind the animal, so that, when he kicked, it would give to the stroke, and would then swing back and hit him, without hurting him; the effect being that the horse would get tired of kicking the inoffensive object, and would, accordingly, drop the habit. If this method be adopted, I would suggest that the animal should, before being left for the night, be accustomed to the stuffed bag, or whatever else is used, touching him. Tying up one fore-leg, or applying the rope-twitch, will keep him quiet while this is being done. I take for granted that he has been, previously, made thoroughly docile, with the exception of this particular vice. The strait-jacket, loosely put on, would, I have no doubt, prevent the kicking. If it was properly applied, and, gradually let out, say, a hole or two, each night, it would, in all probability, break the horse of the habit.

Pawing at night.—I have prevented the practice of this vice by employing a spancel (coupling strap) to connect the animal's fore-legs together, so as to give him freedom to lie down, but not to paw. The use of this strap would, no doubt, in time, cure the vice.

Pawing back the litter.—I note that a correspondent, replying to a query, in the *Field*, as to some means of stopping this practice, which causes the horse to sleep, more or less, on the bare floor, states that connecting the fore-legs in the manner I have just described, will accomplish the object in view, and, after a few repetitions, will wean the animal from the habit.

Rubbing the tail.—Although this vice comes more within the province of the veterinary surgeon, than within that of the breaker, a few remarks on it may not, here, be out of place. Mr. D. C. Pallin, A. V. D., who is a thorough good authority on all matters connected with horses, tells me that he has always found the plan of tying the animal's tail round, with two separate pieces of tape (see Fig. 48)

Fig. 48.—Tail tied with tapes to prevent horse rubbing it.

to be efficacious in stopping the practice of this habit. I may add, that this result may, also, as a rule, be obtained by the application, with the finger, from time to time, of a little blue mercurial ointment, round the inside of the anus. If the rubbing be due to the presence of worms, or to skin disease, appropriate remedies should be employed.

Sleeping standing.—There are many horses that will never, voluntarily, lie down—a habit which seriously detracts from their capacity for work. Such horses might be taught to lie down (see page 153), and, when they had done so, might be kept in the recumbent position by the strait-jacket. Having no experience in this matter, I offer the advice, merely, as a possibly useful suggestion. In all cases, a good, deep bed of straw will be a strong inducement for a horse to lie down.

CHAPTER XVIII.

TEACHING THE HORSE TRICKS.

"Begging"—Bowing—Circling steadily for Circus Work—Coming up to Call—Driving without Reins—Following—Jumping over another Horse, etc.—Kissing—Laughing—Lying down—"No"—Picking up a Handkerchief, etc.—See-sawing on a Plank, etc.—Shaking Hands—Shaking the Head—Waltzing—"Yes."

I MAY mention, that the pluckier a horse is, the more amenable will he be to instruction. In teaching these tricks, it is well to accustom the animal to some invariable and suitable signal, whether vocal, or manual, for each separate feat; and to award his obedience by a piece of carrot, lump of sugar, crust of bread, bite of lucern, bit of sugar-cane, caress, or other appropriate mark of approval.

"*Begging.*"—The horse may be taught to

"beg"—that is, to stand with one fore-leg bent and off the ground—by attaching a strap, or cord, to the pastern of that limb, and, then, pulling up the foot, while at the same time, repeating the word "beg!" After a little, a cutting whip, or cane, to tap the leg, may be substituted for the cord.

Bowing.—While standing at the animal's shoulder, lightly prick him on the breast with a pin; so as to make him bend his neck, and bite at the offending object. He will, thus, soon learn to make his bow, at the mere advance of the hand in the direction of the indicated part.

Circling steadily for circus-work.—Fix the horse's head in position, so as to obtain adequate control, by side-reins; and circle the horse in the ring, with the long reins (see page 172), until he learns to canter round, at a steady, uniform rate of speed. Gradually dispense with the use of the long reins.

Coming up to call.—We may make the horse come up to us, when we call him, in two ways: 1. By getting him to stand still in the manner described on page 86; and making him come up, by threatening him with the whip, alternately, on either side. In this way, he can be taught to come up, by, simply, holding up the whip. 2. By the use of the Comanche bridle (see Figs. 49, 50, and 51), in making the horse turn round towards one, first, at one side, and, then, on the other; always accompanying the pull of the cord, with the words, "Come here!" or some similar expression. Mr. C. G. Frasier taught me this method.

Following.—See preceding paragraph.

Jumping over another Horse, etc.—Let us suppose that we want to make one horse stand perfectly still, and unheld, while another jumps over him. We might, then, adopt the following procedure. Take an enclosed ring, like that of a

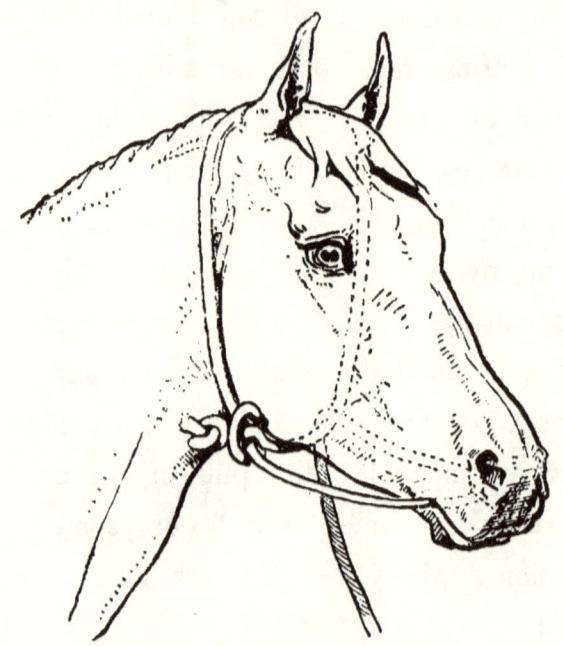

FIG. 49.—Comanche bridle, off side.

circus, and close to its side, and on one of its diameters, construct a trench about 3 feet deep, and 2 feet 6 inches wide, with a ramp leading down to it. Within this trench, place a clothes-horse, or other convenient stand, with rugs over

FIG. 50.—Comanche bridle, near side.

it, and teach, with the long reins (see page 172), the jumper to go round the circle, and jump this stand. We should continue the instruction, until he will jump it without reins. To attain this, when he is loose, we may have to keep on the standing martingale, or use side-reins; so as to

FIG. 51.—The knot on off side of Comanche bridle enlarged.

obtain the necessary control. We may, then, substitute, for the dummy, the real horse, and teach him to stand perfectly still, by means of the rope-twitch (see page 113). All that, now, remains, is to gradually fill up the trench, while continuing the lessons.

Kissing.—This is done by accustoming the horse to take some coveted bit of food out of one's mouth.

Laughing.—This is accomplished in the same way, as a horse is taught to shake his head, by pricking him with a pin, except that, here, the irritation is applied to the muzzle. The horse, thus, learns, on the signal being given, to turn up his upper lip, and shew his teeth. I forget where I, first, saw mention of this trick, which appears to me, neither useful, nor amusing.

Lying down.—Make the horse lie down in the manner described on page 153. When he does so, without offering any resistance, let down the strapped-up leg, and repeat the lesson, until perfect obedience is obtained. We may, then, take off the throwing gear, and make him lie down, by drawing his head round to, say, the near side, with the rein, while standing alongside the off shoulder. The horse will, now, easily learn to lie down, on receiving a signal to do so, by bringing his head round, or, even, by simply saying the words, "Lie down," if they have been employed from the commencement of the teaching. It is, always, well to conduct these lessons on a soft piece of ground with plenty of litter on it; so as to afford the animal an inducement to lie down. Colonel Salkeld of the 2nd Bengal Cavalry has suggested to me the advisability of giving this instruction to army horses, when ordered, after parade, at a time when they are, more or less, tired.

"*No.*"—Take a pin, and prick the horse on the crest with it, until he shakes his head, which he will, readily, do, on that part becoming irritated; as that action is the only means he possesses of getting rid of any annoying object which may pitch on that region. By continuing to touch the horse with the pin, we can make him so sensitive as to shake his head, when touched, only, by the finger; and, finally, even by, merely, raising the hand, which will be a suitable signal to make an animal signify his dissent from a question he may be asked. This is an old circus trick.

Obeying without reins.—Mr. Rockwell, the American horse-tamer, instructed three horses so well, that he was able to drive them together in a trap, and make them moderate their speed, turn, stop, and go on, in perfect obedience, by signals, without reins. Professor Sample used to drive tandem with a leader that did his work without either reins, or traces! The following would be appropriate signals for performing these feats :—" Clicking" with the tongue; for "go on." "Steady"; for "moderate speed." Holding up whip, or saying "whoa!" for "stop." Holding whip to the left, or "left"; for "turn to the left." Holding whip to the right, or "right"; for "turn to the right."

The right-about-turn, and left-about-turn, might be indicated by bringing the whip round, to the right rear, or to the left rear, as the case might be. The signals should be taught the horse by employing them, on all occasions, when using the equivalent indications of the rein, which, to be additionally impressive, should be given sharper than usual.

Picking up a handkerchief, etc.—This is, usually, taught while standing at the horse's side, by pricking him on the ribs with a pin, or pinching him, so as to make him turn round and snap, and, consequently, to seize with his teeth, a handkerchief that is held in a convenient position for him to do so. When he catches hold of the handkerchief, the teacher should take it gently away, and should substitute some appropriate dainty. The horse will, then, soon learn to recognise the fact, that he gets a reward for taking hold of the handkerchief; and, then, can be readily taught to pick it up, or to take it off one of his legs, to which it is loosely tied. Horses that are naturally ticklish, and inclined to snap, are the quickest to learn this trick, in this manner. Instead of getting the horse to catch hold by irritating him, the same object may be obtained by tying up, in the handkerchief, a piece of carrot, or other *bonne bouche*, and inducing the animal to lift up the handkerchief, in his endeavour to get at the contained morsel.

See-sawing on a plank, etc.—Employ the rope-twitch (see Figs. 19-22, pages 108-18), and Comanche bridle (see Figs. 49-51).

Shaking hands.—Teach, as in "begging," *q.v.*, the animal to advance his foot, by pulling it forward.

Shaking the head.—See " No."

Waltzing.—Tie the horse head and tail (see Fig. 45, page 200), and make him go round by flourishing the whip. As the animal obeys, gradually slacken out the cord, until it can be removed.

" *Yes.*"—See " Bowing."

CHAPTER XIX.

TESTING A HORSE'S MANNERS, MOUTH, AND TEMPER.

IF we circle a horse with the long reins (see page 168), turn, jump, and rein him back, we shall be able to form a good idea of his manners, mouth, and temper, by the way in which he goes through his "facings." We may, further, test him, by cracking a whip near him, touching him all over with a long pole, and gently prodding him in the ribs. As a final proof, we may make him lie down, in the manner described on page 153; when it will be easy to see whether he be actuated by a plucky spirit, or by a sullen disposition, which will, always, cause him to adopt a policy of passive resistance. The methods I have here, briefly described, are of great practical value.

CHAPTER XX.

ON IMPROVISED GEAR.

ALTHOUGH I have described in the foregoing pages, a variety of special appliances; still it is well to draw attention to the fact that the whole system of breaking can be carried out with gear which can be improvised without difficulty. We can make a standing martingale with a piece of doubled cord, knotted near the centre to form a loop for the girth to pass through; while the free ends are connected to the rings of the snaffle: or the cord, or strap may be attached to the ring of the breast-plate, in front of the chest; or, as mentioned on page 182, a cord may connect the rings of the standing martingale to those of the snaffle. A stirrup-leather will serve as a leg-strap (see Figs. 14 and 16, pages 101 and 102). Ropes will do for driving reins; a saddle, for a driving-pad (see Figs. 43 and 44, page 185). A head-stall, strong roller, couple of iron rings, crupper, stirrup-leather, pair of knee-caps, and a strong cord, are all that is required for making a horse lie down. An ordinary rope will serve to form a twitch. Any stable rug will do for blindfolding the horse. No special rope is needed for forming a halter, or for noosing a fore-leg. For lifting up a hind-leg, all that we require is a stout cord for the tail, and a stirrup-iron and leather, with which to make a hobble (see Fig. 34, page 144). For driving on foot, we would, of course, want a heavy smooth snaffle. I need hardly say, that a person who wished to go in thoroughly for breaking, ought to provide himself with a driving-pad, or pair of cross-trees, specially made (see Figs. 40 and 41, page 168). Either of these could be made for five-and-twenty shillings. The strait-jacket (see Fig. 25, page 122) is not a necessity.

T

APPENDIX.

COPIES OF TESTIMONIALS, ETC., RECEIVED FROM MEMBERS OF CAPTAIN HAYES' CLASSES.

"BOMBAY, *2nd February*, 1887.

" To

"CAPTAIN M. H. HAYES,

"*Great Western Hotel.*

"DEAR SIR,—I am happy to inform you that the mare you broke for me to riding in September, 1885, still goes quietly. She has not given me any trouble at all since that day. Even when she had not had a saddle on for months, she gave no trouble. As she could not be made to move an inch under the saddle by whip, or spur, or coaxing, before you tried your hand on her, and as you spent only twenty minutes' time on her, I think she is a good proof of the value of your system.

"Yours truly,

"GEO. A. KITTREDGE.

"*Managing Director, Bombay Tramways Company.*"

APPENDIX.

Copy of Testimonial from Captain Hayes' Trimulgherry Class.

TRIMULGHERRY, DECCAN, 8*th November*, 1885.

"We, the undersigned, having on several occasions witnessed Captain Hayes' method of breaking all sorts of horses, have much pleasure in recording our appreciation of its merits. This system of breaking the most nervous or vicious animals is, in our opinion, except with those suffering from some form of disease, invariably efficacious. In addition to the breaking in, Captain Hayes has shewn us many new and very useful points connected with the management of horses. The system is very cheap at the money:—

"C. F. MORTON, COLONEL, 14*th* Hussars.

A. J. ENGLISH, CAPTAIN, 14*th* Hussars.

A. H. WADDEL, *V. S.*, 14*th* Hussars.

T. GRAHAM, RIDING MASTER, 14*th* Hussars.

G. HAMILTON, CAPTAIN, 14*th* Hussars.

C. E. SKYRING HEMERY, LIEUT., 14*th* Hussars.

STUART ROBERTSON, LIEUT., 14*th* Hussars.

R GARTH, MAJOR, 14*th* Hussars.

L. J. RICHARDSON, LIEUT., 14*th* Hussars.

F. J. NORMAN, LIEUT., 14*th* Hussars.

H. W. MITCHELL, LIEUT., 14*th* Hussars.

A. C. KING, CAPTAIN, 14*th* Hussars.

GEO. H. GOUGH, BT., LT.-COL., 14*th Hussars.*

T. MILLER, LIEUTENANT, 14*th* Hussars.

LOFTUS THACKWELL, CAPT., R. Fs., 14*th Hussars.*

F. MUGFORD, *Q. M.*, 14*th* Hussars.

GEO. H. ARBUTHNOT, LIEUT., 3*rd M. L. C.*

F. C. LOGAN-HOME, LIEUT., 3*rd M. L. C.*

J. VANS AGNEW, LIEUT., 3*rd M. L. C.*

C. J. O. FITZGERALD, LT.-COL., 3*rd Cavalry, H. C.*

A. J. GARRETT, *A. A. G., H. C.*

E. NICOLLS, LIEUT., *R. A.*"

The " Pioneer," 18th November, 1885.

CAPTAIN HAYES' HORSE-BREAKING.

To the Editor of the " Pioneer."

Sir,—Captain Hayes is shortly going from this to the Bengal Presidency, and as during his stay he has taught his system of breaking in all sorts of nervous and vicious horses to a large number of people (and horses) here, I shall be much obliged if you can find room in the *Pioneer* for this (and I am but endorsing the opinion of many) my testimony to the excellence of his system. It is most easily acquired, and has only to be seen to be appreciated. His simple method of compelling a refractory horse to enter a railway-box is, in my opinion, alone worth all the money asked for the whole system.

Deccan.   C. F. Morton, Colonel.
14th Hussars.

Copy of Testimonial from Members of Captain Hayes' Calcutta Class.

We, the undersigned, having attended a series of lectures conducted by Captain Hayes on the theory and practice of horse-breaking, hereby certify that Captain Hayes has completely succeeded in all that he promised to effect. We have seen him cure confirmed buck-jumpers and jibbers, so that they were quietly ridden and driven round the school; also savage or nervous horses have speedily been reduced to quietness and obedience. All this had been effected without violence or cruelty. His system appears to us admirable :—

"F. B. Peacock, *C. S.*, Charles H. Moore, W. F. McDonell, *V. C.*, J. J. J. Keswick, } *Stewards, Calcutta Turf Club.*
H. S. Cunningham, *High Court, Calcutta.*
J. Lambert, *Deputy Commissioner of Police.*
F. W. Perman.
S. W. Anderson.
H. B. Beames.
Francis J. E. Spring.
A. Milton.
T. Palmer.
W. D. Kilburn.
P. L. Richards.
H. K. Gordon.
Thos. Brae.
R. John Charlton.
F. Hilton.
J. Lauter, *V. S.*
J. G. Apcar.
F. Aitchison.
J. Posford, *C. S.*
C. Graf.
J. D. Edwards, *A. V. D.*
S. A. Apcar.
F. J. Rowe.
Wm. Macklin.
A. Willson.
Gopee Nauth Roy.

Thos. R. Pratt.
L. P. D. Broughton, *Barrister-at-Law.*
Alex. Campbell.
Wm. Duff Bruce.
A. T. Rawlinson.
Latham Hamilton.
J. J. Reid, *M. D.*
Frank Whitney.
J. Hard.
H. St. A. Goodrich.
S. Keith Douglas.
J. G. Dickson.
Geo. Evans Gordon.
Geo. Cheetham.
A. J. S. Douglas.
Chas. L. Johnstone.
J. D. West.
H. Paget.
Arthur J. C. Forbes.
Kil. Euler.
Robert Philip Heilgers.
J. A. Anderson.
G. Wense.
Charles Brock.
A. R. MacIntosh.
C. Deas.
H. R. McInnes.
J. R. Maples, *Manager, Calcutta Tramways Co.*
John Croft.
R. A. Turnbull, *M.R.C.V.S.*
R. Hardie.

J. A. BOURDILLON, *C. S.*
W. H. EGERTON.
H. MELVILL, *Bo. S. C.*
W. M. BERESFORD.
R. E. S. THOMAS.
WM. CHARLES FOX.
THOMAS A. APCAR.
C. B. JOURDAIN.
J. LEPPOC CAPPEL, *C. S.*
A. L. MCDONELL.

T. A. ST. QUINTON, *Major*, 10*th Hussars.*
O. DIGNUM.
R. C. ONSLOW, 10*th B. Lancers.*
A. A. APCAR.
F. C. BARNES.
CECIL RAWLINSON, CAPTAIN, *L. R.*
F. DE C. H. HELBERT, *R. W., Fusiliers.*
E. V. WESTMACOTT, *C. S.*"

"*Indian Planters' Gazette,*" *9th March*, 1886.

"Regarding a most determined jibber cured by Captain Hayes at Mozufferpore, Mr. Tom Barclay of Bhicanpore writes us as follows:—'I have driven him daily, or rather Colonel Fergus Graham, who has been staying here, has driven him daily for miles, stopping at different places, and starting again, and we have never had any trouble. He trots nicely, and in fact goes as kindly as the most perfect trap horse ever foaled. Captain Hayes may congratulate himself on curing the most vicious, inveterate jibber in India. I tried to sell him in Calcutta for Rs.500, and no one would look at him. Now I would not take Rs.1,500, for he is as fine a trapper as there is in the country.'"

Copy of Testimonial from Captain Hayes' Lucknow Class.

"We, the undersigned, wish to place on record our appreciation of Captain M. H. Hayes' methods of breaking horses of all kinds. The methods are various, and are applicable to all sorts of un-

APPENDIX. 279

broken or refractory horses; most simple in application, and thoroughly efficacious. Some of the subjects submitted to Captain Hayes to test his methods, were as follows :—

"A chestnut waler of E-A., R. H. A., would not allow itself to be mounted, being most violent if mounting it were attempted, in a short time allowed any one to mount and dismount.

"An unbroken remount and bad buck-jumper of 17th Lancers, in the course of two hours, became quiet to ride and perfectly tractable. Ample proof was afforded of the complete control that could be quickly gained over any horse. A stubborn refuser of the 8th B. C. very soon took a delight in jumping; and a confirmed jibber of the 17th Lancers was glad in a short time to move in any direction asked. These few instances we consider convincing proof of the great power of Captain Hayes' system :—

"T. A. COOKE, *Lt.-Col.*, 17*th Lancers*.
B. P. PORTAL, 17*th Lancers*.
H. C. JENKINS, *Capt.*, 17*th Lancers*.
C. D'AGUILAR, 17*th Lancers*.
H. McGEE, *Capt.*, 17*th Lancers*.
S. M. BENSON, *Major*, 17*th Lancers*.
C. COVENTRY, 17*th Lancers*.
A. PORTER, *Capt., B. S. C.*
J. COOK, *Bt. Lt.-Col., A. A. G.*
BARNARD SMITH, *Lt.-Col.*
F. G. POLLOCK, 8*th B. C.*
R. K. RIDGEWAY, *Capt., B. S. C.*
W. P. HARRISON, *Major, G. L. I.*

G. L. EVANS, *C. S.*
G. R. GAMBIER, *Major, R. H. A.*
H. ARCHDALE, *Capt., R. W. Fus.*
H. CHAPMAN, *Col.*, 8*th B. C.*
J. L. ABERIGH-MACKAY, *Capt.*, 8*th B. C.*
R. D. LOUDON, *Capt., R. A.*
S. D. BROWN, *Lieut., R. H. A.*
G. W. BIDDULPH, *Lieut., R. H. A.*
A. H. HEWAT, *Capt., R. H. A.*
P. C. B. PEMBERTON, *Col., R. E.*
H. STEVENSON, *H. L. I.*
CHARSLEY THOMAS, *Lt.-Col.*"

Copy of Report by the Director, Army Remount Operations for India.

"Captain Hayes visited the Saharanpore Army Reserve Remount Depôt on the 16th and 17th of April, 1886, and gave some lectures on horse-breaking, as well as proving by practical demonstration his power of curing horses of nervousness, and rendering them easy to handle. He first of all operated on a bay waler gelding that had only recently arrived from Australia in February last, and would not allow himself to be handled or approached for treatment in hospital.

"In five hours after making him over to him, he was saddled and bridled, and ridden round the school by a Depôt Riding-boy.

"A brown waler mare, which had been five months in the Depôt and would not allow herself to be snaffled or handled in any way, was then taken in hand, and in five hours was able to be saddled, bridled, and ridden about by Captain Hayes' Assistant 'Ted.'

"I am of opinion, and so were those who witnessed his mode of breaking a horse of obstinacy, nervousness, vice, &c., that the treatment he showed us will be a valuable adjunct to those who have executive work to do in Remount Depôts.

"BEN. WILLIAMS, Colonel.

"*Director, Army Remount Operations for India.*"

SAHARANPORE, 20*th April*, 1886.

*Copy of Testimonial from Colonel Truman and Officers,
7th Dragoon Guards.*

"MHOW, CENTRAL INDIA, 21*st January*, 1887.

" Having attended one of Captain Hayes' Classes of Instruction in horse-breaking here, we have much pleasure in testifying to the excellence of the system adopted by him :—

W. R. TRUMAN, LT.-COL., 7*th* Dragoon Guards.
J. H. BANKS, MAJOR, 7*th* Dragoon Guards.
U. G. C. DE BURGH, CAPT., 7*th* Dragoon Guards.
D. MACDOUGAL, CAPT., 7*th* Dragoon Guards.
C. W. THOMPSON, LIEUT., 7*th* Dragoon Guards.
L. A. BROOKS, LIEUT., 7*th* Dragoon Guards.

H. S. FOLLETT, LIEUT., 7*th* Dragoon Guards.
B. R. DIETZ, LIEUT., 7*th* Dragoon Guards.
W. E. DANBY, LIEUT., 7*th* Dragoon Guards.
R. COOPER, LIEUT., 7*th* Dragoon Guards.
W. D. DAUNT, LIEUT., 7*th* Dragoon Guards."

The Calcutta " Englishman," February 19, 1886.

" To the Editor.

" SIR,—In the interests of humanity and in justice to Captain Hayes, who has so successfully introduced his system of taming vicious horses in Calcutta, I hope you will give publicity to the following case of the complete cure of a terribly vicious horse belonging to this company. The horse in question is a roan Kabulee, which has been in our possession, and worked well in a car for over two years, but was so savage that no European could approach him either in or out of his stall. Any attempt to go near him was always met by vigorous striking with his fore feet and biting, generally followed by a rush at the person nearest to him, and an endeavour to get his fore legs over the man's head. He was always dangerous, on one occasion having savaged off a syce's hand, and at another time he took off a man's finger in one vicious snap. On Tuesday afternoon last I took him to Captain Hayes, who, in about an hour, completely cured him, and this without punishment or cruelty of any kind. Two simple, but ingenious contrivances were used, which, without hurting him in any way, prevented him from doing any mischief to those approaching him, and after a few minutes, handling by Captain Hayes, he was pronounced cured, and I was agreeably surprised to find that, on the removal of his gear, he was not only quiet but safe. I must confess to some scepticism at first, as to the performance of the cure, but both yesterday and to-day he is perfectly quiet and tame, and will not only allow Europeans to approach and handle him, but will follow them about the yard when loose. Captain Hayes has clearly demonstrated that jibbers, kickers, buck-jumpers, and extremely nervous horses, can all be cured without even being touched by the whip.

"JNO. R. MAPLES.

"*Managing Agent, Calcutta Tramways Company.*"

Copy of Testimonial from class held in the Royal Artillery Riding School, Woolwich.

"WOOLWICH, *August*, 1887.

"We, the undersigned, having been through a course of Practical Instruction in Lectures given by Captain Hayes on his system of Breaking, Mouthing Horses, and curing them of bad habits, &c., have great pleasure in certifying that we have gained much valuable practical knowledge. Captain Hayes gives such excellent reasons for all he does, that he infuses confidence into those he instructs. With practice any one may use his various methods with the probability of arriving at as great success as himself in the management of horses :—

"S. PARR LYNES, *Col. Supt. Riding Estab.*, *R.A.*
H. H. CROOKENDEN, *Major*, *R.A.*
H. B. JEFFREYS, *Capt. R.H.A.*
C. H. VORES, *Lieut. R.H.A.*
H. MCLAUGHLIN, *Capt. R.A.*

H. ROUSE, *Lieut. R.A.*
H. L. POWELL, *Lieut. R.A.*
CHARLES D. GUINNESS, *Lieut. R.H.A.*
J. ST. L. WHEBLE, *Capt. R.A.*
G. MCMICKING, *Lieut. R.H.A.*
HECTOR CORBYN, *Lieut. R.A.*"

INDEX.

AGGRESSIVENESS, 242
Association of ideas, 12

BALL, DIFFICULT TO, 223
Banham, Mr., 86
Banks and ditches, 187
Bars of the mouth, 46, 65
Baucher, 56
Bearing-reins, 55
Begging, 259
Bending the neck to the rein, 49
Biting, 242
Blew, Mr., 74
Blindfolding, 107
Boring, 216
Bowing, 260
Boy, 10
Bridle, difficult to, 112, 223
Bridle, suitability of horse to the, 46
Bridle twitch, 118
Bridling horse for first time, 171
Buck-jumpers, 203, 222
'Bus horse, 12

CAPPED KNEE, 101
Carrying head and neck, 44
Cart horses, 12
Catch, difficult to, 251

Causes of faults, 2
Chance of doing wrong, 23
" Chancing " fences, 230
Chucking up the head, 217
Circling, 172, 260
Coercion, 23
Collar, 42
Comanche bridle, 262, 263
Coming up to call, 261
Control, horse, 77
Cowkicking, 105
Cruiser, 17
Crupper leading-rein, 148
Curbs, 68

DEFEATS, 20
Defence, 60
Deliberate vice, 3
Difficult to ball, 223
    „   „ bridle, 112
    „   „ catch, 251
    „   „ dismount from, 223
    „   „ drench, 223
    „   „ handle, 223
    „   „ harness, 233
    „   „ mount, 10, 12, 223
    „   „ put into train, 225
    „   „ shoe, 225

INDEX.

Difficult to unharness, 235
Direction of pull of the reins, 50
Dismount from, difficult to, 223
Docile, rendering horses, 147
Dogs, 28
Doing wrong, not getting a chance of, 23
Double hitch Buonaparte bridle, 114
Double sheet-bend, 136
Drench, difficult to, 223
Driving newly-broken horse, 247
Driving pad, 166
Dumb jockeys, 69
" Dwelling " on his stride, 51

ELASTIC REINS, 69
Esa, Mr., 118
Expedition in breaking, 33

FATIGUE, 25
Fanchion, 114, 151
Fence, riding at a, 59
Fences, running out at, 231
„ , rushing at, 232
Field, the, 256
Fighting the horse, 37
Finish of a race, 51
Fire, unsteady under, 226
First step, 32
Fixing hind quarters, 60
Following, 261
Foreleg, holding up, 96
„ , lifting up, 93, 94, 96
„ , taking up, 88
„ , tying up, 99, 102
Frasier, Mr., 113

GAGGING A HORSE, 143
Gag, wooden, 145
Gateacre, Colonel, 143
" Game," nervous horses not, 6
Gear, improvised, 272
Gentling hind leg, 135
Gentling neck, 81, 88
Gentling the horse, 151
Going level, 51
Good hands, 65
Good mouth chief requirement, 30
Groom, 28, 29
Ground, keeping horse on the, 157

HALTERING, PRATT'S METHOD OF, 86
Halter, rope, 78
Halter twitch, 108
Haltering loose horse, 80
Hamilton, 153
Hands, good, 65
Handle, difficult to, 223
Hanging against the pole, 236
„ on the headstall, 251
Handkerchief, picking up a, 268
Hard pulling, 66
Harness, breaking to, 212
„ , difficult to, 233
„ , faults in, 233
„ , lying down in, 240
„ , plunging when starting in, 241
Head and neck, carrying the, 44
Head and tail, tying the, 197, 206
Head, chucking up the, 217
„ , position of the, 66
Headstall, hanging on the, 251
Headstall twitch, 117, 118

Hickman, Colonel, 74, 249
Hind-leg, gentling, 135
„   „ , lifting up, 126, 135
Hind-quarters, fixing, 60
Hippo-lasso, 119
Hobble, improvising a, 143
Holding horse down, 165
Holding up fore-leg, 96
Horse-breaking, object of, 1
„   „ , scope of, 14
„   „ , value of, 14
Horse-control, 77
How it is done, 32

IDIOCY, 21
Improvised gear, 272
Instinct, 7
Intelligence of the horse, 9

JIBBING, 18, 19, 60, 227, 236
Jump, teaching to, 188
Jumping faults, 230
Jumping over another horse, 261
Jumping too slowly, 230

KEEPING A HORSE ON THE GROUND, 157
Kemp, Mr., 217
Kicker, touching a, 7
Kicking, 238, 244, 252
Kicking at night, 252
Kicking from nervousness, 4
Kindness, 36
Kissing, 265

LADIES' HORSES, BREAKING, 209
Laughing, 265
Leach, Mr., 96

Leading-rein, crupper, 148
Leg, outward, 56
Leg strap, Rarey's, 99
„   „ , stirrup leather, 105
Lie down, making a horse, 153
Lifting up fore-leg, 93, 94, 96
„   „ hind-leg, 126
Linguist, 10
Litter, pawing back the, 256
Log for jumping, 188
Loose horse, haltering, 80
Lunging, 64
Lying down, 265
Lying down in harness, 240

MAGNER, 151, 218
Making horse lie down, 153
Manners, testing, 271
Martingale, running, 52
„   , standing, 70
Mathematician, 10
Memory of the horse, 9
Mental qualities of the horse, 7
Methods of breaking, various, 29
Military exigencies, 34
„   riding, 52
Mitchell, Mr., 239
Moore, Mr. J. H., 174, 190, 249
Mount, difficult to, 12, 223
Mounting, Australian method, 204
„   horse for first time, 197
Mouth, 30
„   , faults of, 216
„   , testing, 271
Mouthing gear, 166
„   , on foot, 172
„   , principles of, 41
Mouth-piece, action of, 47

Muscles of the neck, 44, 45
Mutton fist, 67

NECK, GENTLING, 81, 88
Neck muscles, 44, 45
Neck, scratching the, 81
Nervousness, 3, 18, 226
Newmarket, 65, 179
Night, kicking at, 252
„ , pawing at, 256
" No ! ", 266
Noosing fore-leg, 93
Nose-bands, 76

OBEYING THE REIN, 41
Obeying without reins, 265
Obey, making horse, 37
Object of horse-breaking, 1
Ordinary method of breaking, 35
Outward leg, 56

PAD, DRIVING, 166
Pallin, Mr., 224, 256
Pawing at night, 256
Pawing back the litter, 256
Peat, General, 146
Permanency of breaking, 31, 35
Personal influence, 28
Petting horses, 10
Plunging when starting in harness, 241
Pole, gentling with the, 81 88, 93
„ , hanging against the, 236
„ , pulling away from the, 241
Polo, savaging at, 245
„ , shying off the ball at, 220
Possibility of overcoming any vice, 16

Pratt, Mr., 113, 151, 218
Pratt's method of haltering, 86
„ twitch, 113
Principle of rendering horses docile, 38
Pulling, 66, 218
Pulling away from the pole, 241
„ successfully, 42
Punishment, 24

QUICK BREAKING, 33
Quiet to ride, 37

RAABE AND LUNEL, 119
Racing snaffle, thin, 69
Ranks, refusing to quit the, 229
Rarey, 15, 17
Rareyfying, 24
Rarey's leg strap, 99
Rawlins, Colonel, 93
Rearing, 60, 219
Reasoning, 8, 17
Refusing, 231
Rein-bearers, 171
Rein, getting tail over the, 235
Reining back, 63
Rein, obeying the, 41
Reins, 171
Reins, pull of the, 50
Rideable and driveable, 22
Riding newly-broken horse, 247
River, 13
Rockwell, Mr., 151, 267
Rope-halter, 78
Rope-twitch, 113
„ „ , advantages of, 112
Rough and ready method, 37
Rubbing the tail, 256

INDEX.

Running martingale, 52
Running out at fences, 231
Running reins, 55
Rushing at fences, 232

SADDLING HORSE FOR FIRST TIME, 171
Salkeld, Colonel, 266
Sample, Professor, 19, 22, 190, 208, 267
Saunders, Mr., 102
Savage, young, 39
Savaging, 244
Savaging at polo, 245
Saving the mouth, 49, 50, 67, 68
Scope of breaking, 14
Scratching horse's neck, 81
See-sawing on a plank, 269
Self-preservation, 10
Shaking hands, 269
Shaking the head, 270
Sheet bend, double, 136
Shoe, difficult to, 225
Short tail, tying rope to, 143
Shying, 220
Shying off the ball at polo, 220
Side reins, 55
Sleeping standing, 258
Snaffles, 68
Spoiled horses, 34, 36
Sprinter bar, tying tail to, 240
Stable vices, 251
Standing behind breaker, 78
Standing martingale, 70
Stand still, making horse, 86
Stargazing, 53, 220
"Steady!", 111
Stirrup leather for leg strap, 105

Strait jacket, 118
  „   „   , throwing with the, 152
Striking out in front, 246
Stubbornness, 18
Suitability of horse to bridle, 47
Sulking, 158
Sulky horse, 24
Sword, unsteady with a, 220

TAIL OVER THE REIN, GETTING THE, 235
Tail, rubbing the, 256
Tail, short, 143
  „ to sprinter bar, tying, 240
  „ with tape, tying, 257
Taking up fore-leg, 88
  „   „   hind-leg, 126
Tape, tying tail with, 257
Teaching horses tricks, 10, 259
Temper, testing, 271
Tender mouthed, 220
Testing manners, 271
  „   mouth, 271
  „   temper, 271
Then and there, 36
Thin racing snaffle, 69
Throwing with strait jacket, 152
Tiring in the gallop, 51
Touched, nervous of being, 226
Touching a kicker, 7
Train, difficult to put into, 225
Turn, difficult to, 221
  „ , teaching to, 56
Turning, 59
Twitch, bridle, 118
  „ , headstall, 117, 118
  „ , ordinary, 112, 113
  „ , Pratt's, 113

U

Twitch, rope, 113
Tying up fore-leg, 99, 102

UNHARNESS, DIFFICULT TO, 235

VALUE OF BREAKING, 14
Various methods, 29
Vice, deliberate, 3
Vice in the horse, 3
Vices, 20
,, , stable, 251
Voice, 27

WALTZING, 270
Wardrop, Colonel, 74, 182
Whip, undue fear of, 241
,, , unsteady with the, 226
White's Veterinary Art, 54
Without reins, obeying, 267

"YAWING," 221
"Yes," 270
Yield, making the horse, 11
Young horses, 43
,,   savage, 39

Capt. M. H HAYES'

BOOKS ON HORSES.

Capt. Hayes' Books on Horses.

NEW EDITION.

VETERINARY HINTS FOR HORSE-OWNERS.

A Handbook of Veterinary Medicine and Surgery, written in popular language. Fourth Edition, Revised and Enlarged, with Additional Illustrations. Crown 8vo. 10s. 6d.

[*In the press.*

" Of the many popular veterinary books which have come under our notice, this is certainly one of the most scientific and reliable. Some notice is accorded to nearly all the diseases which are common to horses in this country, and the writer takes advantage of his Indian experience to touch upon several maladies of horses in that country, where veterinary surgeons are few and far between."—*The Field.*

"The work is written in a clear and practical way."—*Saturday Review.*

"The book leaves nothing to be desired on the score of lucidity and comprehensiveness."—*Veterinary Journal.*

"The present edition is nearly double the size of the first one, and the additional articles are well and clearly written, and much increase the value of the work. We do not think that horse-owners in general are likely to find a more reliable and useful book for guidance in an emergency."—*The Field.*

RIDING: on the Flat and Across Country.

A Guide to Practical Horsemanship. Illustrated by STURGESS. Third Edition, Revised and Enlarged. Imperial 16mo. 10s. 6d. [*In the press.*

"The book is one that no man who has ever sat in a saddle can fail to read with interest."—*Illustrated Sporting and Dramatic News.*

" A master of his subject."—*Standard.*

" An excellent book on riding."—*Truth.*

" It has, however, been reserved for Captain Hayes to write what in our opinion will be generally accepted as the most comprehensive, enlightened, and 'all round' work on riding; bringing to bear, as he does, not only his own great experience, but the advice and practice of many of the best recognized horsemen of the period."—*The Sporting Life.*

"An eminently practical teacher, whose theories are the outcome of experience, learned not in the study, but on the road, in the hunting-field, and on the racecourse."—*Baily's Magazine.*

Capt. Hayes' Books on Horses.

HORSE TRAINING AND MANAGEMENT IN INDIA.

Fourth Edition, Revised. Crown 8vo. 8s. 6d.

"We entertain a very high opinion of Captain Hayes' book on Horse Training and Management in India, and are of opinion that no better guide could be placed in the hands of either amateur horseman or veterinary surgeon newly arrived in that important division of our empire."—*The Veterinary Journal.*

"A useful guide in regard to horses anywhere. . . . Concise, practical, and portable."—*Saturday Review.*

"We have always been able to commend Captain Hayes' books as being essentially practical, and written in understandable language. As trainer, owner, and rider of horses on the flat and over country, the author has had a wide experience, and when to this is added competent veterinary knowledge, it is clear that Captain Hayes is entitled to attention when he speaks."—*The Field.*

ILLUSTRATED HORSE BREAKING IN THEORY AND PRACTICE.

With 52 Plates by J. H. OSWALD BROWN. Uniform with "Riding." 21s.

SOUNDNESS AND AGE OF HORSES.

A Veterinary and Legal Guide to the Examination of Horses for Soundness. By Capt. M. H. HAYES. With upwards of 100 Illustrations. Crown 8vo. 8s. 6d.

"'Soundness and Age of Horses' is more technical, and shows that Captain Hayes has not confined his experiences of horses to the mere riding of them. All who have horses to buy, sell, or keep, will find plenty to interest them in this manual, which is full of illustrations, and still fuller of hints and 'wrinkles.'"—*The Referee.*

"Captain Hayes' work is evidently the result of much careful research, and the horseman, as well as the veterinarian, will find in it much that is interesting and instructive."—*The Field.*

Capt. Hayes' Books on Horses.

INDIAN RACING REMINISCENCES.

Being Anecdotes of Men, Horses, and Sport. Illustrated with Twenty-two Portraits and a number of smaller Engravings. Imperial 16mo. 8s. 6d.

"All sportsmen who can appreciate a book on racing, written in a chatty style and full of anecdote, will like Captain Hayes' latest work. In this book, as in his others, Captain Hayes shows himself a thorough master of his subject, and has so skilfully interwoven technicalities, history, and anecdote, that the last page comes all too soon."—*The Field.*

"No racing reminiscences have ever been recorded so graphically, with such a loving lingering over the days that were, and with such a wide personal acquaintance with the horses, the men, and the times, as Captain Hayes has done in his new book."—*The Indian Planter's Gazette.*

A MANUAL OF PRACTICAL TACTICS.

Crown 8vo. 6s.

"Captain Hayes' book deals exclusively with tactics, and is a well-considered treatise on that branch of the art of war, giving not merely rules, but also principles and reasons. We would particularly draw attention to the chapter on the defensive, which subject is treated with more fulness than is usually found in English books. . . . A valuable chapter on machine-guns winds up the work."—*The Times.*

IN PREPARATION.

THE HORSEWOMAN. A Practical Guide for Ladies in the Art of Riding. Illustrated. By M. H. and A. M. HAYES. Imperial 16mo.

THE POINTS OF THE HORSE. A Familiar Treatise on Equine Conformation. Describing the Points in which the perfection of each class of Horses consists. Illustrated by numerous Drawings from Photographs and exact measurements of Living Typical Animals. Illustrated by J. H. OSWALD BROWN. Oblong 4to.

No. 60.   January, 1894.

A SELECT CATALOGUE OF WORKS,
CHIEFLY ILLUSTRATED, PUBLISHED
BY W. THACKER & CO.,
87 NEWGATE STREET, LONDON, AND
THACKER, SPINK & CO,
CALCUTTA.

BANIAN TREE.

TO BE OBTAINED ALSO OF

THACKER & CO., LIMITED, BOMBAY.

THE IMAGE OF WAR: Service on the Chin Hills. By SURGEON-CAPTAIN A. G. E. NEWLAND.

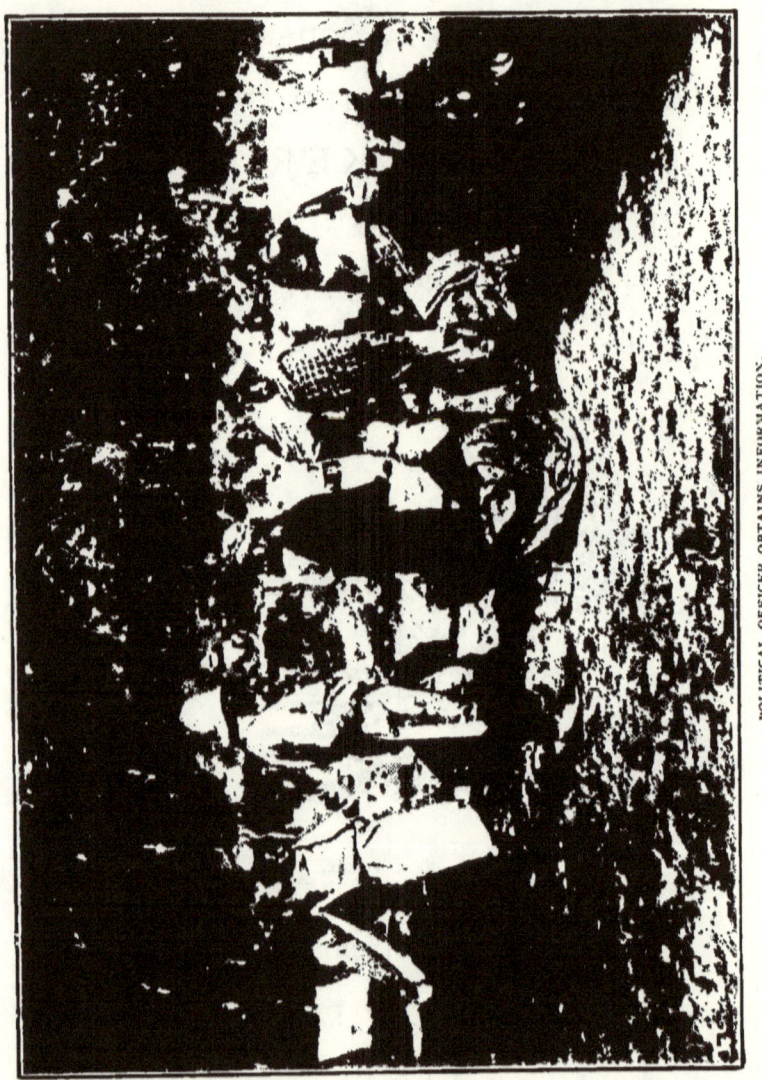

POLITICAL OFFICER OBTAINS INFORMATION.

194 Illustrations from Instantaneous Photographs. Demy 4to. £1 11s. 6d.

Messrs. THACKER, SPINK & CO. will shortly publish a work unique in its character and extremely beautiful in its form, entitled,

THE IMAGE OF WAR; or, Service on the Chin Hills.
BY SURGEON-CAPTAIN A. G. E. NEWLAND.

With an Introductory Historical Note by J. D. MACNABB, ESQ., *Political Officer, South Chin Hills.* Demy 4to.

POLITICAL OFFICER RECEIVING SUBMISSION OF TASHON CHIEFS.

It is illustrated by 34 full-page Collotypes of Instantaneous Photographs, and 160 interspersed in the reading. No work has yet appeared, in Europe or America, of this beautiful character. The price to subscribers is *Rs.* 25, but as only a small edition is printed, Messrs Thacker, Spink & Co. hold themselves at liberty to raise the price upon publication to *Rs.* 30. From its nature the book cannot be reprinted, and subscribers will possess a work of extreme beauty, interest and rarity.

A NATURALIST ON THE PROWL.

PYTHON CRUSHING MONKEY. (FROM INSTANTANEOUS PHOTOGRAPH.)

By EHA, Author of "Tribes on my Frontier," etc.

In the Press, a new work by that popular writer, EHA, Author of "THE TRIBES ON MY FRONTIER," and "BEHIND THE BUNGALOW," called

A NATURALIST ON THE PROWL.

Profusely Illustrated by Drawings by Mr. R. A. STERNDALE, F.R.G.S., F.Z.S., Author of "Mammalia of India," "Denizens of the Jungle," "Seonee," etc., who has studied and sketched animals of all kinds in their habitat and at work.

JACKAL ON THE PROWL.

EHA cannot be dull, and the book will not only be uniform with the former popular works, but fully equal in interest and life.

THACKER, SPINK & CO., CALCUTTA.

Fifth Edition. In Imperial 16mo, uniform with "Lays of Ind," "Riding," "Hindu Mythology," etc. 8s. 6d.

THE TRIBES ON MY FRONTIER:
An Indian Naturalist's Foreign Policy.
By EHA.
WITH FIFTY ILLUSTRATIONS BY F. C. MACRAE.

N this remarkably clever work there are most graphically and humorously described the surroundings of a Mofussil bungalow. The twenty chapters embrace a year's experiences, and provide endless sources of amusement and suggestion. The numerous able illustrations add very greatly to the interest of the volume, which will find a place on every table.

THE CHAPTERS ARE—

I.—A Durbar.
II.—The Rats.
III.—The Mosquitos.
IV.—The Lizards.
V.—The Ants.
VI.—The Crows.
VII.—The Bats.
VIII.—Bees, Wasps, et hoc genus omne.
IX.—The Spiders.
X.—The Butterfly: Hunting Him.

XI.—The Butterfly: Contemplating Him.
XII.—The Frogs.
XIII.—The Bugs.
XIV.—The Birds of the Garden.
XV.—The Birds at the Mango Tope.
XVI.—The Birds at the Tank.
XVII.—The Poultry Yard.
XVIII.—The White Ants.
XIX.—The Hypodermatikosyringophoroi.
XX.—Etcetera.

W. THACKER & CO., LONDON.

THE TRIBES ON MY FRONTIER.

Fifth Edition. 8s. 6d.

"It is a very clever record of a year's observations round the bungalow in 'Dustypore.' . . . . It is by no means a mere travesty. . . . . The writer is always amusing, and never dull."—*Field.*

"The book is cleverly illustrated by Mr. F. C. Macrae. We have only to thank our Anglo-Indian naturalist for the delightful book which he has sent home to his countrymen in Britain. May he live to give us another such."— *Chambers's Journal.*

"A most charming series of sprightly and entertaining essays on what may be termed the fauna of the Indian bungalow. . . . . We have no doubt that this amusing book will find its way into every Anglo-Indian's library."— *Allen's Indian Mail.*

"This is a delightful book, irresistibly funny in description and illustration, but full of genuine science too. . . . . . There is not a dull or uninstructive page in the whole book."—*Knowledge.*

"It is a pleasantly-written book about the insects and other torments of India which make Anglo-Indian life unpleasant, and which can be read with pleasure even by those beyond the reach of the tormenting things Eha describes."—*Graphic.*

"The volume is full of accurate and unfamiliar observation."
—*Saturday Review.*

THACKER, SPINK & CO., CALCUTTA.

Fourth Edition, Imperial 16mo. 6s.

BEHIND THE BUNGALOW.
By EHA,
AUTHOR OF "TRIBES ON MY FRONTIER."

WITH FIFTY-THREE CLEVER SKETCHES
By the Illustrator of "The Tribes."

As "The Tribes on my Frontier" graphically and humorously described the Animal Surroundings of an Indian Bungalow, the present work describes with much pleasantry the Human Officials thereof, with their peculiarities, idiosyncrasies, and, to the European, strange methods of duty. Each chapter contains Character Sketches by the Illustrator of "The Tribes," and the work is a "Natural History" of the Native Tribes who in India render us service.

W. THACKER & CO., LONDON.

"There is plenty of fun in 'Behind the Bungalow,' and more than fun for those with eyes to see. These sketches may have an educational purpose beyond that of mere amusement; they show through all their fun a keen observation of native character and a just appreciation of it."
—*The World.*

BEHIND THE BUNGALOW.
By the Author of "TRIBES ON MY FRONTIER."
AND ILLUSTRATED BY THE SAME ARTIST.

"'The Tribes On My Frontier' was very good: 'Behind the Bungalow' is even better. Anglo-Indians will see how truthful are these sketches. People who know nothing about India will delight in the clever drawings and the truly humorous descriptions; and, their appetite for fun being gratified, they will not fail to note the undercurrent of sympathy."
—*The Graphic.*

"The native members of an Anglo-Indian household are hit off with great fidelity and humour."—*The Queen.*

LAYS OF IND. By Aliph Cheem.
COMIC, SATIRICAL, AND DESCRIPTIVE
Poems Illustrative of Anglo-Indian Life.
ILLUSTRATED BY THE AUTHOR, LIONEL INGLIS, R. A. STERNDALE, AND OTHERS.

Ninth Edition. Cloth, gilt. 10s. 6d.

"This is a remarkably bright little book. 'Aliph Cheem,' supposed to be the *nom de plume* of an officer in the 18th Hussars, is, after his fashion, an Indian Bon Gaultier. In a few of the poems the jokes, turning on local names and customs, are somewhat esoteric ; but, taken throughout, the verses are characterized by high animal spirits, great cleverness, and most excellent fooling."—*The World.*

"One can readily imagine the merriment created round the camp fire by the recitation of 'The Two Thumpers,' which is irresistibly droll. . . . The edition before us is enlarged, and contains illustrations by the author, in addition to which it is beautifully printed and handsomely got up, all which recommendations are sure to make the name of Aliph Cheem more popular in India than ever."—*Liverpool Mercury.*

"Satire of the most amusing and inoffensive kind, humour the most genuine, and pathos the most touching pervade these 'Lays of Ind.' . . . From Indian friends we have heard of the popularity these 'Lays' have obtained in the land where they were written, and we predict for them a popularity equally great at home."—*Monthly Homœopathic Review.*

W. THACKER & CO., LONDON.

Reviews of "Lays of Ind."

"The 'Lays' are not only Anglo-Indian in origin, but out-and-out Anglo-Indian in subject and colour. To one who knows something of life at an Indian 'station' they will be especially amusing. Their exuberant fun at the same time may well attract the attention of the ill-defined individual known as 'the general reader.'"—*Scotsman.*

"To many Anglo-Indians the lively verses of 'Aliph Cheem' must be very well known, while to those who have not yet become acquainted with them we can only say read them on the first opportunity. To those not familiar with Indian life they may be specially commended for the picture which they give of many of its lighter incidents and conditions, and of several of its ordinary personages."—*Bath Chronicle.*

Seventh Edition. In square 32mo. 5s.

DEPARTMENTAL DITTIES AND OTHER VERSES.
Humorous and Character Poems of Anglo-Indian Life.
By RUDYARD KIPLING.

"They reflect with light gaiety the thoughts and feelings of actual men and women, and are true as well as clever. . . . Mr. Kipling achieves the feat of making Anglo-Indian society flirt and intrigue visibly before our eyes. . . . His book gives hope of a new literary star of no mean magnitude rising in the East."
—SIR W. W. HUNTER, *in The Academy.*

"As for that terrible, scathing piece, 'The Story of Uriah,' we know of nothing with which to compare it, and one cannot help the wretched feeling that it is true. . . . 'In Spring Time' is the most pathetic lament of an exile we know in modern poetry."—*Graphic.*

RHYMING LEGENDS OF IND
By H. K. GRACEY, B.A., C.S.   *Crown 8vo, 6s.*

"A series of lively Stories in Verse."—*Times.*

"Are not only amusing but are lively descriptions of scenery and customs in Indian Life. . . . Cleverly and humorously told."—*Weekly Times.*

THACKER, SPINK & CO., CALCUTTA.

Crown 8vo. 6s.

COW KEEPING IN INDIA.
A simple and practical book on

Their care and treatment, their various breeds,

AND

THE MEANS OF RENDERING THEM PROFITABLE.

BY ISA TWEED.

CROWN 8vo.

With Thirty-Nine Illustrations, including the various Breeds of Cattle, drawn from Photographs by

R. A. STERNDALE.

W. THACKER & CO., LONDON.

NEARLY READY.

DOGS FOR HOT CLIMATES.

By VERO SHAW.

Author of Cassell's "Book of the Dog." Late Kennel Editor of the "Field."

AND

CAPTAIN M. H. HAYES, F.R.C.V.S.

Author of "Veterinary Notes," etc.

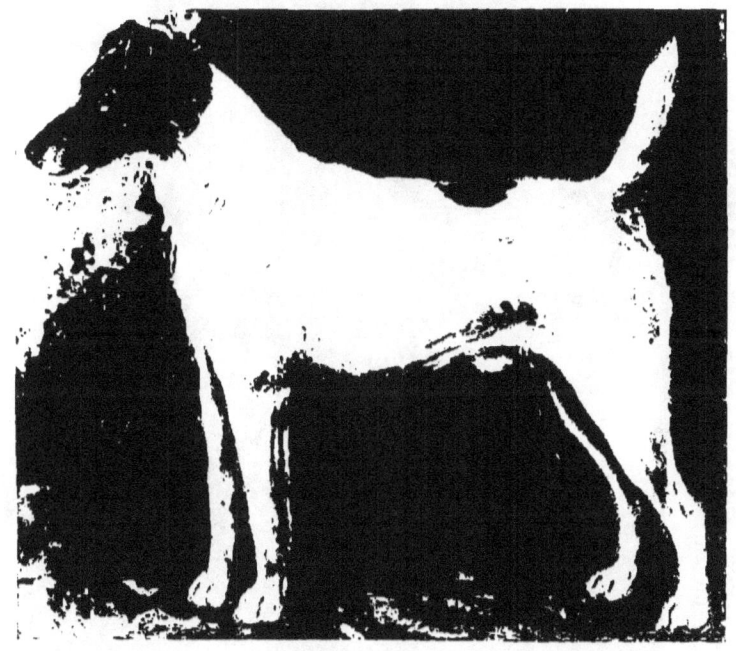

The book will be illustrated by typical animals of each breed treated of, chiefly from Photographs of Prize Winners, and will be essential to all lovers of the Dog in Hot Climates. It will be uniform with "Cow Keeping in India," "Poultry Keeping in India," etc.

POULTRY KEEPING IN INDIA. A Simple and Practical Book on their Care and Treatment: their various Breeds, and the means of rendering them profitable. In Crown 8vo. Illustrated.

By ISA TWEED, Author of "Cow Keeping in India."

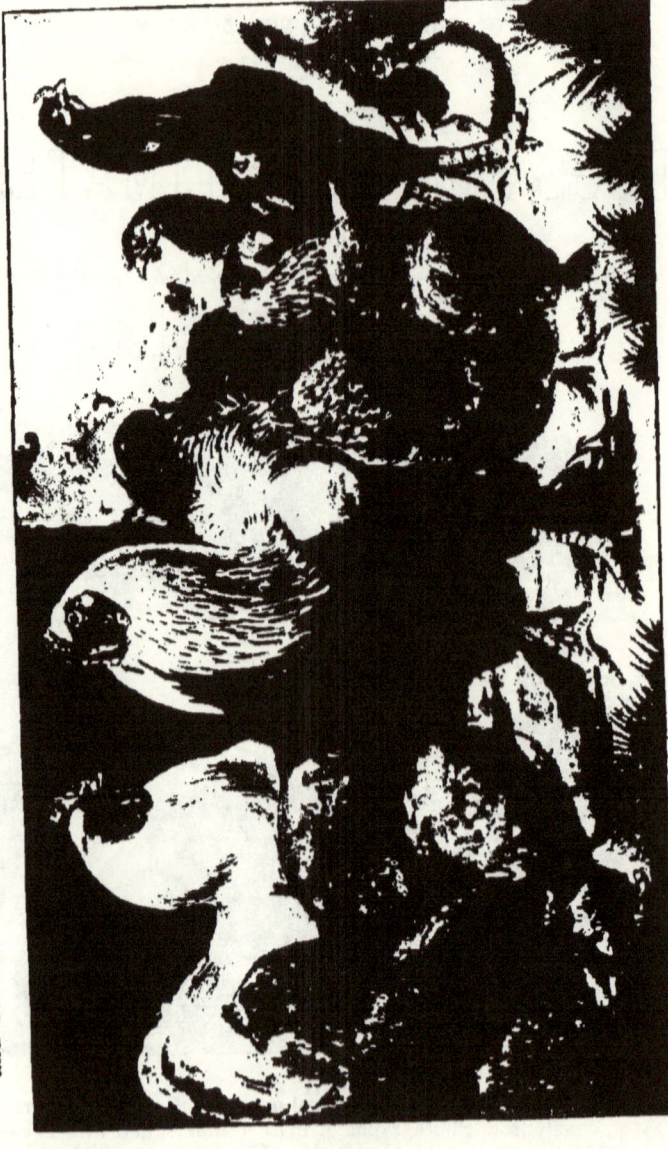

W. THACKER & CO., LONDON.

The Second Edition, Revised, and with additional Illustrations by the Author.
Post 8vo. 8s. 6d.

SEONEE:
OR,
CAMP LIFE ON THE SATPURA RANGE.
A Tale of Indian Adventure.

By R. A. STERNDALE,
AUTHOR OF "MAMMALIA OF INDIA," "DENIZENS OF THE JUNGLE."

Illustrated by the Author.

With an Appendix containing a brief Topographical and Historical account of the District of Seonee in the Central Provinces of India.

THACKER, SPINK & CO., CALCUTTA.

In Imperial 16mo. Uniform with " Riding," " Riding for Ladies," " Hindu Mythology." 12s. 6d.

A NATURAL HISTORY
OF THE
MAMMALIA OF INDIA,
BURMAH AND CEYLON.

By R. A. STERNDALE, F.R.G.S., F.Z.S., ETC.,

AUTHOR OF "SEONEE," "THE DENIZENS OF THE JUNGLE," "THE AFGHAN KNIFE," ETC.

WITH 170 ILLUSTRATIONS BY THE AUTHOR AND OTHERS.

The geographical limits of the present work have been extended to all territories likely to be reached by the sportsman from India. It is copiously illustrated, not only by the author himself, but by careful selections made by him from the works of well-known artists.

"It is the very model of what a popular natural history should be."—*Knowledge*.
"An amusing work with good illustrations."—*Nature*.
"Full of accurate observation, brightly told."—*Saturday Review*.
"The results of a close and sympathetic observation."—*Athenæum*.
"It has the brevity which is the soul of wit, and a delicacy of allusion which charms the literary critic."—*Academy*.
"The notices of each animal are, as a rule, short, though on some of the larger mammals—the lion, tiger, pard, boar, etc.—ample and interesting details are given, including occasional anecdotes of adventure. The book will, no doubt, be specially useful to the sportsman, and, indeed, has been extended so as to include all territories likely to be reached by the sportsman from India. Those who desire to obtain some general information, popularly conveyed, on the subject with which the book deals, will, we believe, find it useful."—*The Times*.
"Has contrived to hit a happy mean between the stiff scientific treatise and the bosh of what may be called anecdotal zoology."—*The Daily News*.

W. THACKER & CO., LONDON.

Foolscap 8vo, with 8 Maps. *Rs.* 3-8.

THE SPORTSMAN'S MANUAL

IN QUEST OF GAME

IN KULLU, LAHOUL AND LADAK, TO THE TSO MORARI LAKES.

WITH NOTES ON SHOOTING IN SPITI, BARA BAGAHAL, CHAMBA AND KASHMIR;
AND A DETAILED DESCRIPTION OF SPORT IN MORE THAN 130 NALAS.

BY

LIEUT.-COL. R. H. TYACKE.

LATE H.M.'S 98TH AND 34TH REGIMENTS.

Oblong Imperial 4to. 16s.

DENIZENS OF THE JUNGLES:

A Series of Sketches of Wild Animals,

ILLUSTRATING THEIR FORMS AND NATURAL ATTITUDES. WITH LETTERPRESS
DESCRIPTION OF EACH PLATE.

BY R. A. STERNDALE, F.R.G.S., F.Z.S.,

AUTHOR OF "NATURAL HISTORY OF THE MAMMALIA OF INDIA," "SEONEE," ETC.

1. Denizens of the Jungles.—*Aborigines—Deer—Monkeys.*
2. On the Watch.—*Tiger.*
3. Not so fast Asleep as he Looks.—*Panther—Monkeys.*
4. Waiting for Father.—*Black Bears of the Plains.*
5. Rival Monarchs. — *Tiger and Elephant.*
6. Hors de Combat.—*Indian Wild Boar and Tiger.*
7. A Race for Life. — *Blue Bull and Wild Dogs.*
8. Meaning Mischief.—*The Gaur—Indian Bison.*
9. More than His Match.—*Buffalo and Rhinoceros.*
10. A Critical Moment. — *Spotted Deer and Leopard.*
11. Hard hit—*The Sambur.*
12. Mountain Monarchs. — *Marco Polo's Sheep.*

"The plates are admirably executed by photo-lithography from the author's originals, every line and touch being faithfully preserved. It is a volume which will be eagerly studied on many a table. Many an amusing and exciting anecdote add to the general interest of the work."—*Broad Arrow.*

"The Volume is well got up and the drawings are spirited and natural."—*Illustrated London News.*

THACKER, SPINK & CO., CALCUTTA.

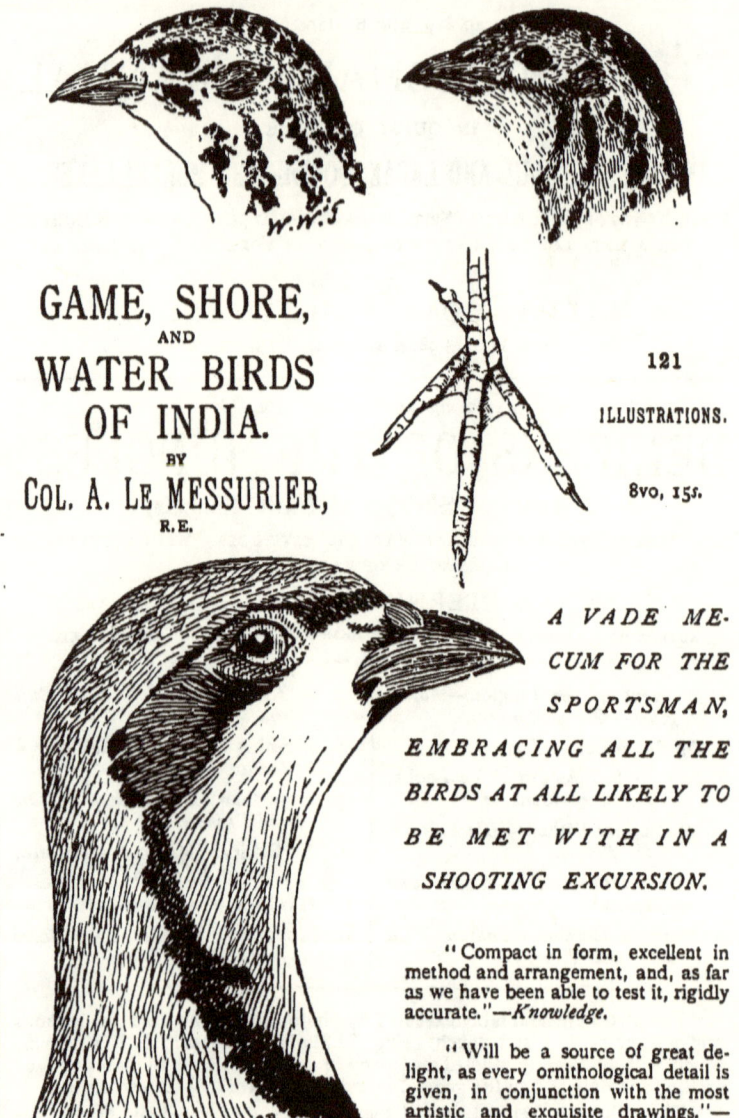

GAME, SHORE,
AND
WATER BIRDS OF INDIA.
BY
Col. A. Le MESSURIER,
R. E.

121 ILLUSTRATIONS.

8vo, 15s.

A VADE ME-CUM FOR THE SPORTSMAN, EMBRACING ALL THE BIRDS AT ALL LIKELY TO BE MET WITH IN A SHOOTING EXCURSION.

"Compact in form, excellent in method and arrangement, and, as far as we have been able to test it, rigidly accurate."—*Knowledge.*

"Will be a source of great delight, as every ornithological detail is given, in conjunction with the most artistic and exquisite drawings."—*Home News.*

W. THACKER & CO., LONDON.

"Splendidly Illustrated Record of Sport."—*Graphic.*

Third Edition. Enlarged. Demy 4to. 36 Plates and Map. £2 2s.

LARGE GAME SHOOTING
IN THIBET, THE HIMALAYAS, NORTHERN & CENTRAL INDIA.
By Brig.-General ALEX. A. A. KINLOCH.

Reduced size.

"Colonel Kinloch, who has killed most kinds of Indian game, small and great, relates incidents of his varied sporting experiences in chapters, which are each descriptive of a different animal. The photo-gravures of the heads of many of the animals, from the grand gaur, popularly miscalled the bison, downwards, are extremely clever and spirited."—*Times.*

THACKER, SPINK & CO., CALCUTTA.

New Edition, Demy 8vo, with all Original Illustrations. Rs. 7-8.

The Highlands of Central India.
NOTES ON THEIR
Forests and Wild Tribes, Natural History and Sport.

By CAPT. J. FORSYTH, BENGAL STAFF CORPS.
WITH
ILLUSTRATIONS BY R. A. STERNDALE, F.Z.S., F.R.G.S.

In Demy folio, Thirty-nine Plates, Natural Size. 25s.

ILLUSTRATIONS OF THE
Grasses of the Southern Punjab.
BEING
Photo-Lithographs of some of the Grasses found at Hissar, with Descriptive Letterpress.

By WILLIAM COLDSTREAM, B.A., B.C.S.

W. THACKER & CO., LONDON.

Fourth Edition, Crown 8vo, Buckram. 12s. 6d.

VETERINARY NOTES FOR HORSE-OWNERS.

An Illustrated Manual of Horse Medicine and Surgery, written in Simple Language.

BY CAPT. M. H. HAYES, F.R.C.V.S.

"Captain Hayes' work is a valuable addition to our stable literature; and the illustrations, tolerably numerous, are excellent beyond the reach of criticism."—*Saturday Review.*

"The description of symptoms and proper methods of treatment in sickness render the book a necessary guide for horseowners, especially those who are far removed from immediate professional assistance."—*The Times.*

"Of the many popular veterinary books which have come under our notice, this is certainly one of the most scientific and reliable. If some painstaking student would give us works of equal merit to this on the diseases of the other domestic animals, we should possess a very complete veterinary library in a very small compass."—*Field.*

"Simplicity is one of the most commendable features in the book. What Captain Hayes has to say he says in plain terms, and the book is a very useful one for everybody who is concerned with horses."—*Illustrated Sporting and Dramatic News.*

"The usefulness of the manual is testified to by its popularity, and each edition has given evidence of increasing care on the part of the author to render it more complete and trustworthy as a book of reference for amateurs."—*The Lancet.*

"A volume replete with most interesting information, couched in the simplest terms possible."—*The County Gentleman.*

"The book leaves nothing to be desired on the score of lucidity and comprehensiveness."—*Veterinary Journal.*

THACKER, SPINK & CO., CALCUTTA.

Square 8vo, 10s. 6d.
THE HORSEWOMAN.
A PRACTICAL GUIDE TO SIDE-SADDLE RIDING.

BY MRS. HAYES.   EDITED BY CAPTAIN M. H. HAYES.

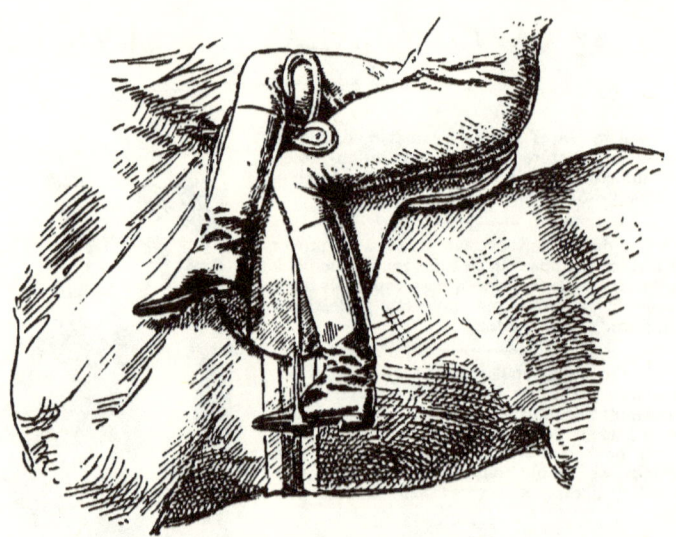

With 4 Collotypes from Instantaneous Photographs, and 48 Drawings after Photographs, by J. H. OSWALD BROWN.

PRESS NOTICES.

The Times.—" A large amount of sound, practical instruction, very judiciously and pleasantly imparted."

The Field.—" This is the first occasion on which a practical horseman and a practical horsewoman have collaborated in bringing out a book on riding for ladies. The result is in every way satisfactory, and, no matter how well a lady

W. THACKER & CO., LONDON.

THE HORSEWOMAN.

PRESS NOTICES.—(*Continued.*)

may ride, she will gain much valuable information from a perusal of 'The Horsewoman.' The book is happily free from self-laudatory passages."

The Athenæum.—"We have seldom come across a brighter book than '*The Horsewoman.*'

The Queen.—"A most useful and practical book on side-saddle riding, which may be read with real interest by all lady riders."

Freeman's Journal (Dublin).—"Mrs. Hayes is perhaps the best authority in these countries on everything connected with horsemanship for ladies."

Scotsman (Edinburgh).—"The work is the outcome of experiences, aptitudes, and opportunities wholly exceptional."

Le Sport (Paris).—"J'ai lu ou parcouru bien des traités d'équitation usuelle ou savante ; jamais encore je n'avais trouvé un exposé aussi clair, aussi simple, aussi vécu que celui où Mme. Hayes résume les principes dont une pratique assidue lui a permis d'apprécier la valeur. Ce très remarquable manuel d'equitation féminine est bien, comme la desire son auteur, à la portée de tous et il est à souhaiter qu'il trouvé en France l'accueil et le succès qu'il à rencontrés dès sa publication auprès des horsewomen anglaises."

Saturday Review.—"With a very strong recommendation of this book as far and away the best guide to side-saddle riding that we have seen."

The Queen.—"It is a real pleasure to see a lady ride as Mrs. Hayes does ; she combines in an unusual degree an absolutely firm, strong seat with a pretty and graceful one.'

Land and Water.—"A more thorough horsewoman than Mrs. Hayes probably does not exist."

Hearth and Home.—"The Duke of Cambridge personally complimented her on her seat and hands."

Indian Planters' Gazette (Calcutta).—"The victory [in jumping competition] was well earned. Mrs. Hayes treated the large crowd to an exhibition of horsemanship, the like of which has seldom, if ever, been witnessed in Calcutta. The merit of the performance is enhanced by the fact that she had never ridden the mare before that day."

The Mining Argus (Johannesburg, Transvaal).—"Mrs. Hayes is undoubtedly one of the pluckiest and most accomplished horsewomen we have ever seen."

North China Daily News (Shanghai).—"This accomplished horsewoman practically illustrated, for the benefit of the ladies present, what she wrote in our columns about riding without reins, even over stiff jumps, on a mount only broken for a lady ten minutes before."

THACKER, SPINK & CO., CALCUTTA.

Third Edition, Imperial 16mo.   10s. 6d.

RIDING:
ON THE FLAT AND ACROSS COUNTRY.
A Guide to Practical Horsemanship.

BY CAPTAIN M. H. HAYES, F.R.C.V.S.

The Times.—" Captain Hayes' hints and instructions are useful aids, even to experienced riders, while for those less accustomed to the saddle, his instructions are simply invaluable."

The Standard.—" Captain Hayes is not only a master of his subject, but he knows how to aid others in gaining such a mastery as may be obtained by the study of a book."

The Field.—"We are not in the least surprised that a third edition of this useful and eminently practical book should be called for. On former occasions we were able to speak of it in terms of commendation, and this edition is worthy of equal praise."

Baily's Magazine.—"An eminently practical teacher, whose theories are the outcome of experience, learned not in the study, but on the road, in the hunting field, and on the racecourse."

Sporting Times.—" We heartily commend it to our readers."

Illustrated Sporting and Dramatic News.—" The book is one that no man who has ever sat in a saddle can fail to read with interest."

The Graphic.—" Is as practical as Captain Horace Hayes' 'Veterinary Notes' and 'Guide to Horse Management in India.' Greater praise than this it is impossible to give."

Uniform with "Riding," etc. 21s.

ILLUSTRATED HORSE-BREAKING

BY

Capt. M. H. HAYES.

1. Theory of Breaking.
2. Principles of Mounting.
3. Horse Control.
4. Rendering Docile.
5. Giving Good Mouths.
6. Teaching to Jump.
7. Mounting for First Time.
8. Breaking for Ladies' Riding.
9. Breaking to Harness.
10. Faults of Mouth.
11. Nervousness and Impatience of Control.
12. Jibbing.
13. Jumping Faults.
14. Faults in Harness.
15. Aggressiveness.
16. Riding and Driving Newly-broken Horse.
17. Stable Vices.
18. Teaching Circus Tricks.

"The work is eminently practical and readable."—*Veterinary Journal*.

"Clearly explained in simple, practical language, made all the more clear by a set of capital drawings."—*Scotsman*.

"It is characteristic of all Captain Hayes' books on Horses that they are eminently practical, and the present one is no exception to the rule. A work which is entitled to high praise as being far and away the best reasoned-out book on Breaking under a new system we have seen."—*Field*.

WITH FIFTY-ONE ILLUSTRATIONS BY J. H. OSWALD BROWN.

THACKER, SPINK & CO., CALCUTTA.

Foolscap 4to, 34s.
THE POINTS OF THE HORSE.
A familiar treatise on Equine Conformation.
By Capt. M. H. HAYES, F.R.C.V.S.

DESCRIBING THE POINTS IN WHICH THE PERFECTION OF EACH CLASS OF HORSES CONSISTS.

Illustrated by 76 *reproductions of Photographs of Typical Horses, and* 204 *Drawings, chiefly by* J. H. OSWALD BROWN.

W. THACKER & CO., LONDON.

THE POINTS OF THE HORSE.

Times. — "An elaborate and instructive compendium of sound knowledge on a subject of great moment to all owners of horses, by a writer of established authority on all matters connected with the horse."

Army and Navy Gazette. —"It is scientific in its method, and practical in its purpose."

Nature.—"A soldier, a certificated veterinarian, a traveller and a successful rider, the author is well qualified to treat on all that pertains to the subject before us."

The Referee.—"What Captain Hayes does not know about horses is probably not particularly worth knowing."

Saturday Review.—"This is another of Captain Hayes' good books on the horse, and to say it is the best would not be going far out of the way of truth. It is a luxurious book, well got up, well and clearly printed in large readable type and profusely illustrated."

Pall Mall Budget.—"A volume that must be regarded as the standard work on the subject. It is well done. No point is left unexplained; no quality in a type unnoticed."

Sporting Times.—"The best production of its kind we have seen."

Field.—"To those who are desirous of availing themselves of the knowledge of a writer who has been used to horses all his life, the book may be cordially recommended."

Veterinary Journal.—"No book like this has hitherto appeared in English, or any other language. For giving us such a beautiful, interesting and instructive book, the members of the veterinary profession, horsemen and horse owners, as well as delineators of the horse, in every English speaking country must acknowledge themselves deeply indebted to Captain Hayes."

THACKER, SPINK & CO., CALCUTTA.

In Imperial 16mo. Illustrated. 8s. 6d.

INDIAN RACING REMINISCENCES:
BEING

ENTERTAINING NARRATIVES AND ANECDOTES OF MEN, HORSES, AND SPORT.

Illustrated with Twenty-Two Portraits and a Number of Smaller Engravings.

By CAPTAIN M. HORACE HAYES.

"The book is full of racy anecdote, and the author writes so kindly of his brother officers and the sporting planters with whom he came into contact, that one cannot help admiring the genial and happy temperament of the author."—*Bell's Life.*

"Captain Hayes shows himself a thorough master of his subject, and has so skilfully interwoven technicalities, history, and anecdote, that the last page comes all too soon."—*Field.*

Fifth Edition. Revised. Crown 8vo. 9s.

TRAINING & HORSE MANAGEMENT IN INDIA.

By CAPTAIN M. HORACE HAYES, F.R.C.V.S.

"No better guide could be placed in the hands of either amateur horseman or veterinary surgeon."—*The Veterinary Journal.*

"A useful guide in regard to horses anywhere. Concise, practical, and portable."—*Saturday Review.*

W. THACKER & CO., LONDON.

Crown 8vo.   Uniform with "Veterinary Notes."   8s. 6d.

SOUNDNESS AND AGE OF HORSES.

WITH ONE HUNDRED AND SEVENTY ILLUSTRATIONS.

A Complete Guide to all those features which require attention when purchasing Horses, distinguishing mere defects from the symptoms of unsoundness; with explicit instructions how to conduct an examination of the various parts.

BY CAPTAIN M. H. HAYES, F.R.C.V.S.

"Captain Hayes is entitled to much credit for the explicit and sensible manner in which he has discussed the many questions—some of them extremely vexed ones—which pertain to soundness and unsoundness in horses."—*Veterinary Journal.*

"Captain Hayes' work is evidently the result of much careful research, and the horseman, as well as the veterinarian, will find in it much that is interesting and instructive."—*Field.*

THACKER, SPINK & CO., CALCUTTA.

In Imperial 16mo. Uniform with "Lays of Ind," "Hindu Mythology," etc.
Handsomely bound. 10s. 6d.

RIDING FOR LADIES.
With Hints on the Stable.
BY MRS. POWER O'DONOGHUE.
AUTHOR OF "LADIES ON HORSEBACK," "A BEGGAR ON HORSEBACK," etc.

With 91 Illustrations drawn expressly for the Work by A. Chantrey Corbould.

HIS able and beautiful volume will form a Standard on the Subject, and is one which no lady can dispense with. The scope of the work will be understood by the following:

CONTENTS.
I. Ought Children to Ride?
II. "For Mothers & Children."
III. First Hints to a Learner.
IV. Selecting a Mount.
V., VI. The Lady's Dress.
VII. Bitting.   VIII. Saddling.
IX. How to Sit, Canter, &c.
X. Reins, Voice, and Whip.
XI. Riding on the Road.
XII. Paces, Vices, and Faults.
XIII. A Lesson in Leaping.
XIV. Managing Refusers.
XV. Falling.
XVI. Hunting Outfit Considered.

XVII. Economy in Riding Dress.	XX. Shoeing. XXI. Feeding.
XVIII. Hacks and Hunters.	XXII. Stabling. XXIII. Doctoring.
XIX. In the Hunting Field.	XXIV. Breeding. XXV. "Tips."

"When there may arise differences of opinion as to some of the suggestions contained in this volume, the reader, especially if a woman, may feel assured she will not go far astray in accepting what is said by one of her own sex, who has the distinction of three times beating the Empress of Austria in the hunting field, from whom she 'took the brush.' 'Riding for Ladies' is certain to become a classic."
—*New York Sportsman.*

W. THACKER & CO., LONDON.

Crown 8vo. 7s. 6d.
A TEA PLANTER'S LIFE IN ASSAM.
By GEORGE M. BARKER.
WITH 75 ILLUSTRATIONS.

This book aims at conveying to all interested in India and the tea industry an entertaining and useful account of the topographical features of Assam; the strange surroundings—human and animal—of the European resident; the trying climate; the daily life of the planter; and general details of the formation and working of tea gardens.

"Mr. Barker has supplied us with a very good and readable description, accompanied by numerous illustrations drawn by himself. What may be called the business parts of the book are of most value."—*Contemporary Review.*

"Cheery, well-written little book."—*Graphic.*

"A very interesting and amusing book, artistically illustrated from sketches drawn by the author."—*Mark Lane Express.*

LIST OF THE TEA GARDENS OF INDIA AND CEYLON.
Their Acreage, Managers, Assistants, Calcutta Agents, Coolie Depôts, Proprietors, Companies, Directors, Capital, London Agents and Factory Marks, by which any chest may be identified. Also embraces Coffee, Indigo, Silk, Sugar, Cinchona, Lac, Cardamom and other Concerns. 8vo. Sewed. 6s.

"The strong point of the book is the reproduction of the factory marks, which are presented side by side with the letterpress. To buyers of tea and other Indian products on this side, the work needs no recommendation."—*British Trade Journal.*

THACKER, SPINK & CO., CALCUTTA.

Crown 8vo. 7s. 6d.

THE INDIGO MANUFACTURER.

A Practical and Theoretical Guide

FROM THE RECEIPT OF THE PLANT TO THE PRODUCTION OF THE CAKE;

With numerous EXPERIMENTS Illustrating the Scientific Principles bearing on each Phase of the Manufacture.

By J. BRIDGES-LEE, M.A., F.C.S., F.Z.S., F.R.A.S. Bengal, etc., etc.

"It enlightens us on a matter about which our knowledge till now has been highly barren and uncertain—the technicalities of the winning of the Indigo from its Indian home. Each operation which the Indigo has to undergo before its perfection has a separate chapter. At the end of each, experiments are described which are to serve this purpose, so that the object for which the pourtrayed operation is given is made clear and put in a right light."—*Chemiker Zeitung* (Translated).

In Crown 8vo. 7s. 6d.

THE CULTURE AND MANUFACTURE OF INDIGO:

WITH DESCRIPTION OF A PLANTER'S LIFE AND RESOURCES.

By W. M. REID.

WITH NINETEEN ILLUSTRATIONS BY THE AUTHOR.

"A concise and readable manual, not only of everything relating to the industry, but of the whole round of business and recreation that makes up the Planter's life. . . . The writer is at once accurate and graphic, and on the strength merely of reading these bright pages one almost feels competent to take full charge of a 'concern.'"—*Englishman.*

W. THACKER & CO., LONDON.

Uniform with "Lays of Ind,' "Riding," etc. 10s. 6d.

HINDU MYTHOLOGY:
VEDIC AND PURANIC.

BY

REV. W. J. WILKINS,
OF THE LONDON MISSIONARY
SOCIETY, CALCUTTA.

Illustrated by One Hundred Engravings chiefly from Drawings by Native Artists

REVIEWS.

"His aim has been to give a faithful account of the Hindu deities such as an intelligent native would himself give, and he has endeavoured, in order to achieve his purpose, to keep his mind free from prejudice or theological bias. To help to completeness he has included a number of drawings of the principal deities, executed by native artists. The author has attempted a work of no little ambition and has succeeded in his attempt, the volume being one of great interest and usefulness; and not the less so because he has strictly refrained from diluting his facts with comments of his own. It has numerous illustrations."—*Home News.*

"Mr. Wilkins has done his work well, with an honest desire to state facts apart from all theological prepossession, and his volume is likely to be a useful book of reference."—*Guardian.*

"In Mr. Wilkins' book we have an illustrated manual, the study of which will lay a solid foundation for more advanced knowledge, while it will furnish those who may have the desire without having the time or opportunity to go further into the subject, with a really extensive stock of accurate information."—*Indian Daily News.*

H. E. BUSTEED'S "ECHOES FROM OLD CALCUTTA."

A MOST INTERESTING SERIES OF SKETCHES OF CALCUTTA LIFE, CHIEFLY TOWARDS THE CLOSE OF THE LAST CENTURY. Second Edition. Post 8vo. Rs. 6. (8s. 6d.) With Numerous Illustrations.

Door of Black Hole. Grated Windows.

THE "BLACK HOLE" OF CALCUTTA.

"It is a pleasure to reiterate the warm commendation of this instructive and lively volume which its appearance called forth some few years since. It would be lamentable if a book so fraught with interest to all Englishmen should be restricted to Anglo-Indian circles. A fresh instalment of letters from Warren Hastings to his wife must be noted as extremely interesting, while the papers on Sir Philip Francis, Nuncomar, and the romantic career of Mrs. Grand, who became Princess Benevento and the wife of Talleyrand, ought to be widely known."—*Saturday Review.*

"Dr. Busted has unearthed some astonishing revelations of what European Life in India resembled a century back."—*Daily Telegraph.*

W. THACKER & CO., LONDON.

300 Illustrations.   Imperial 16mo.   12s. 6d.

A HANDBOOK OF INDIAN FERNS.
By COLONEL R. H. BEDDOME, F.L.S.,
Late Conservator of Forests, Madras.

"It is the first special book of portable size and moderate price which has been devoted to Indian Ferns, and is in every way deserving of the extensive circulation it is sure to obtain."—*Nature.*

"I have just seen a new work on Indian Ferns which will prove vastly interesting, not only to the Indian people, but to the botanists of this country."—*Indian Daily News.*

"The 'Ferns of India.' This is a good book, being of a useful and trustworthy character. The species are familiarly described, and most of them illustrated by small figures."—*Gardeners' Chronicle.*

"Those interested in botany will do well to procure a new work on the 'Ferns of British India.' The work will prove a first-class text book."—*Free Press.*

3s. 6d.

SUPPLEMENT to the FERNS OF BRITISH INDIA, etc.
By COLONEL R. H. BEDDOME.
Containing Ferns which have been discovered since the publication of "The Handbook to the Ferns of British India," etc.

NEARLY READY.

HOW TO CHOOSE A DOG, & HOW TO SELECT A PUPPY.
TOGETHER WITH A FEW NOTES UPON THE PECULIARITIES AND CHARACTERISTICS OF EACH BREED.

By VERO SHAW,
Author of "The Illustrated Book of the Dog," late Kennel Editor of the "Field."

This small work will give in a brief, yet compendious form, the various Breeds—their Characteristics—Points—Average Weights at various Ages from six weeks to full growth—Points to look for in choosing average age at which the breed arrives at maturity, etc. The book is prepared in response to the innumerable inquiries showered upon the Author in his editorial capacity, and will form an invaluable guide in the selection of Dogs, as well as an aide-memoir to all.

Crown 8vo. Illustrated. *Rs.* 5; Interleaved, *Rs.* 5-8.

A TEXT BOOK
OF
INDIAN BOTANY:
MORPHOLOGICAL,
PHYSIOLOGICAL,
and SYSTEMATIC.

By W. H. GREGG,
Lecturer on Botany, Hughli College.

With 240 Illustrations.

Crown 8vo. 7s. 6d. Illustrated.

MANUAL OF
AGRICULTURE FOR INDIA.
By Lieut. F. POGSON.

---

1. Origin and Character of Soils.—2. Ploughing and Preparing for Seed.—3. Manures and Composts.—4. Wheat Cultivation.—5. Barley.—6. Oats.—7. Rye.—8. Rice.—9. Maize.—10. Sugar-producing Sorghums.—11. Common Sorghums.—12. Sugarcane.—13. Oil Seed.—14. Field Pea Crops.—15. Dall or Pulse.—16. Root Crops.—17. Cold Spice.—18. Fodder.—19. Water-Nut.—20. Ground-Nut.—21. Rush-Nut or Chufas.—22. Cotton.—23. Tobacco.—24. Mensuration.—Appendix.

"A work of extreme practical value."—*Home News.*

"Mr. Pogson's advice may be profitably followed by both native and European agriculturists, for it is eminently practical and devoid of empiricism. His little volume embodies the teaching of a large and varied experience, and deserves to be warmly supported."—*Madras Mail.*

W. THACKER & CO., LONDON.

Fourth Edition, Imperial 16mo.   15s.   Illustrated.

A MANUAL OF GARDENING
FOR
BENGAL AND UPPER INDIA.
By THOMAS A. C. FIRMINGER, M.A.
THOROUGHLY REVISED AND BROUGHT DOWN TO THE PRESENT TIME BY
J. H. JACKSON,
Editor of "The Indian Agriculturist."

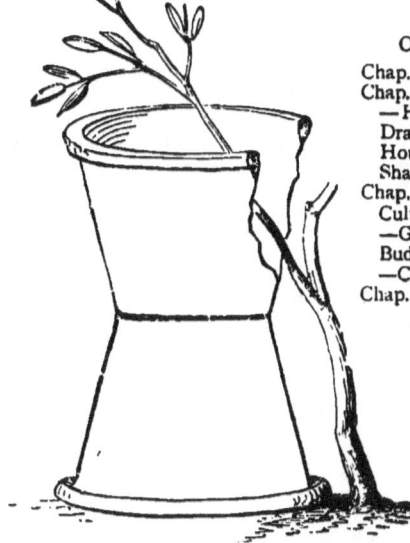

PART I.
OPERATIONS OF GARDENING.
Chap. I.—Climate—Soils—Manures.
Chap. II.—Laying-out a Garden—Lawns —Hedges—Hoeing and Digging— Drainage — Conservatories — Betel Houses—Decorations—Implements— Shades—Labels—Vermin—Weeds.
Chap. III.—Seeds—Seed Sowing—Pot Culture—Planting—Cuttings—Layers —Gootee—Grafting and Inarching— Budding—Pruning and Root Pruning —Conveyance.
Chap. IV.—Calendar of Operations.

PART II.
GARDEN PLANTS.
1. Culinary Vegetables.
2. Dessert Fruits.
3. Edible Nuts.
4. Ornamental Annuals.
5. Ornamental Trees, Shrubs, and Herbaceous Perennials.

Crown 8vo, cloth.   *Rs.* 2-8.

THE AMATEUR GARDENER IN THE HILLS.
HINTS FROM VARIOUS AUTHORITIES ON GARDEN MANAGEMENT,
AND ADAPTED TO THE HILLS;
WITH HINTS ON FOWLS, PIGEONS, AND RABBIT KEEPING;
And various Recipes connected with the above subjects which are not commonly found in Recipe Books.

THACKER, SPINK & CO., CALCUTTA.

Thacker's Guide Books.

Agra and its Neighbourhood: A Handbook for Visitors. By H. G. KEENE, C.S. Fifth Edition, Revised. Maps, Plans, &c. Fcap. 8vo, cloth. *Rs.* 2-8.

Allahabad, Cawnpore and Lucknow. By H. G. KEENE, C.S. Second Edition, Re-written and Enlarged. Fcap. 8vo.

Burma and its People, Manners, Customs and Religion. By Capt. C. J. V. S. FORBES. 8vo. *Rs.* 4 (7*s.* 6*d.*).

Burmah Myam-Ma: the Home of the Burman. By TSAYA (Rev. H. POWELL). Crown 8vo. *Rs.* 2 (3*s.* 6*d.*).

Calcutta, Thacker's Guide to. With Chapters on its Bypaths, &c., and a Chapter on the Government of India. Fcap. 8vo. With Maps. *Rs.* 3.

Calcutta to Liverpool by China, Japan and America, in 1877. By Lieut.-General Sir HENRY NORMAN. Second Edition. Fcap. 8vo, cloth. *Rs.* 2-8 (3*s.* 6*d.*).

Darjeeling and its Neighbourhood. By S. MITCHELL, M.A. With two Maps. *Rs.* 2.

Delhi and its Neighbourhood, A Handbook for Visitors to. By H. G. KEENE, C.S. Third Edition. Maps. Fcap. 8vo, cloth. *Rs.* 2-8.

India, Thacker's Map, in case, 8*s.* 6*d.*

India, Map of the Civil Divisions of; including Governments, Divisions and Districts, Political Agencies and Native States; also the Cities and Towns. *Re.* 1.

Kashmir Handbook (Ince's). Revised and Re-written. By Surg.-Major JOSHUA DUKE. With 4 Maps. Fcap. 8vo, cloth. *Rs.* 6-8.

Kashgaria (Eastern or Chinese Turkestan), Historical, Geographical, Military and Industrial. By Col. KUROPATKIN, Russian Army. Translated by Major GOWAN, H. M.'s Indian Army. 8vo. *Rs.* 6-8.

Kumaun Lakes, Angling in the. With a Map of the Kumaun Lake Country. By Depy. Surg.-Genl. W. WALKER. Crown 8vo, cloth. *Rs.* 4.
"Written with all the tenderness and attention to detail which characterise the followers of the gentle art."—*Hayes' Sporting News.*

Lucknow, Tourists' Guide to. Plans. *Rs.* 2.

Masuri, Landaur, Dehra Dun, and the Hills North of Dehra; including Routes to the Snows and other places of note; with chapter on Garhwal (Tehri), Hardwar, Rurki, and Chakrata. By JOHN NORTHAM. *Rs.* 2-8.

Simla, The Hills beyond. Three Months' Tour from Simla ("In the Footsteps of the Few") through Bussahir, Kunowar, and Spiti, to Lahoul. By Mrs. J. C. MURRAY-AYNSLEY. Crown 8vo, cloth. *Rs.* 3.

Gold, Copper and Lead in Chota Nagpore. Compiled by Dr. W. KING, Director Geological Survey of India, and T. A. POPE, Dep. Supt. Survey of India. With Map of Geological Formation and the Areas taken up by the various Prospecting and Mining Companies. Crown 8vo, cloth. *Rs.* 5.

Russian Conversation-Grammar (on the System of Otto). With Exercises, Colloquial Phrases, and an English-Russian Vocabulary. By A. KINLOCH, late Interpreter to H.B.M. Consulate, St. Petersburg. 9*s.*
On the system of Otto, with Illustrations, phrases and idioms; leading by easy and rapid gradations to a colloquial knowledge of the Language.

W. THACKER & CO., LONDON.

The Reconnoitrer's Guide and Field Book, adapted for India. By Major M. J. KING-HARMAN, B.S.C. Third Edition, Revised and in great part re-written. In roan. *Rs.* 4.
Can be used as an ordinary Pocket Note Book, or as a Field Message Book; the pages are ruled as a Field Book, and in sections, for written description or sketch. "To officers serving in India this guide will be invaluable."—*Broad Arrow.*

Tales from Indian History: being the Annals of India retold in Narratives. By J. TALBOYS WHEELER. Sixth Edition. Crown 8vo, cloth gilt. 3s. 6d.

Hindustani as it ought to be Spoken. A Manual with Explanations, Vocabularies and Exercises. By J. TWEEDIE, C.S. Second Edition. *Rs.* 2-8.

A Memoir of the late Justice Onoocool Chunder Mookerjee. By M. MOOKERJEE. Third Edition, 12mo. *Re.* 1.
A most interesting and amusing illustration of Indian English.
"The reader is earnestly advised to procure the life of this gentleman, written by his nephew, and read it."—*The Tribes on my Frontier.*

The Indian Cookery Book. A Practical Handbook to the Kitchen in India: adapted to the Three Presidencies. By a Thirty-five Years' Resident. *Rs.* 3.

Indian Notes about Dogs: their Diseases and Treatment. By Major C——. Third Edition, Revised. Fcap. 8vo, cloth. *Rs.* 1-8.

Indian Horse Notes: an Epitome of useful Information. By Major C——, Author of "Indian Notes about Dogs." Second Edition, Enlarged. Fcap. 8vo, cloth. *Rs.* 2.

Horse-Breeding and Rearing in India: with Notes on Training for the Flat and Across Country; and on Purchase, Breaking-in, and General Management. By Major J. HUMFREY. Crown 8vo. *Rs.* 3-8.

Hygiene of Water and Water Supplies. By PATRICK HEHIR, M.D., F.R.C.S. Edin.; Lecturer on Hygiene, Hyderabad. Surgeon, Bengal Army. 8vo, limp cloth. *Rs.* 2.

Plain Tales from the Hills: A Collection of Stories by RUDYARD KIPLING. Third Edition. Crown 8vo. *Rs.* 4.
"They sparkle with fun; they are full of life, merriment and humour."—*Allen's Indian Mail.*

A Text Book of Medical Jurisprudence for India. By I. B. LYON, C.I.E., F.G.S., F.I.C. Professor of Chemistry and Medical Jurisprudence Grant, Medical College, Bombay. Revised, as to the Legal Matter, by J. D. INVERARITY, Advocate of the High Court, Bombay. Medium 8vo. Illustrated. 25s.

The Management and Medical Treatment of Children in India. By EDWARD A. BIRCH, M.D., Surg.-Major, Bengal Establishment. Second Edition Revised (cing the Eighth Edition of "Goodeve's Hints"). Crown 8vo. 10s. 6d.

Our Administration of India. Being a Complete Account of the Revenue and Collectorate Administration in all Departments, with special reference to the Work and Duties of a District Officer in Bengal. By H. A. D. PHILLIPS. 6s.

The Indian Medical Service. A Guide for intended Candidates and for the Junior Officers of the Service. By W. W. WEBB, M.B., Bengal Army. Crown 8vo. *Rs.* 4.

Thacker's Indian Directory. Embracing the whole Territories under the Viceroy, with the Native States. Published Annually. 36s.

INDEX.

		Page
"Amateur Gardener in the Hills." ... Rs. 2-8	...	37
Barker. "Tea Planter in Assam."	7/6	31
Beddome. "Ferns of India."	12/6	35
Birch. "Children in India."	10/6	39
Bridges-Lees. "Indigo Manufacturer."	7/6	32
Busteed. "Echoes from Old Calcutta"	8/6	34
Coldstream. "Grasses of the Punjab."	25/-	29
Eha. "Behind the Bungalow."	6/-	8
,, "Tribes on my Frontier."	8/6	6
,, "A Naturalist on the Prowl."	...	4
Firminger. "Gardening for India." By Jackson.	15/-	37
Forsyth. "Highlands of Central India." ,, 7-8	...	20
Gracey. "Rhyming Legends of Ind."	6/-	11
Gregg. "Indian Botany." ,, 5	...	36
Guide Books.	...	38
Hayes. "Veterinary Notes." ... 12/6 "Riding."	10/6	21-24
,, "Horsewoman." ... 10/6 "Illustrated Horse-Breaking."	21/-	22-25
,, "Points of the Horse." ... "Soundness and Age."	8/	26-29
,, "Indian Racing." ... 8/6 "Training and Management."	1/	28
Hehir. "Hygiene of Water." ,, 2	4/(	39
Humfrey. "Horse-Breeding." ,,	...	39
"Indian Cookery." ,,.	4/6	39
"Indian Notes—Dogs." ,, 1-8	...	39
"Indian ,, Horses." ,, 2	...	39
King and Pope. "Gold, Copper, Lead," &c. ,, 5	...	38
King-Harman. "Reconnoitring." ,, 4	...	39
Kinloch. "Large Game."	42/-	19
,, "Russian Grammar."	9/-	38
Kipling. "Plain Tales." ,, 4	...	39
,, "Departmental Ditties."	5/-	11
"Lays of Ind." By Aliph Cheem.	10/6	10
Le Messurier. "Game Birds."	15/-	18
Lyon. "Medical Jurisprudence."	25/-	39
Newland. "Image of War."	...	2
O'Donoghue. "Riding for Ladies."	10/6	30
"Onoocool Mookerjee, Life of." ,, 1	...	39
Phillips. "Our Administration of India."	6/-	39
Pogson. "Agriculture for India."	7/6	36
Reid. "Indigo Planter."	7/6	32
Shaw. "Dogs for Hot Climates."	...	13
,, "How to Choose a Dog," etc.	...	35
Sterndale. "Denizens of the Jungle."	16/-	17
,, "Mammalia of India."	12/6	16
,, "Seonee."	8/6	15
"Tea Gardens of India and Ceylon."	6/6	31
Thacker's Guide Books, various.	...	38
,, "Indian Directory.'	36/-	39
,, "Map of India.	8/6	38
Tweedie. "How to Speak Hindustani. ,, 2-8	...	39
Tweed. "Cow Keeping in India."	6/-	12
,, "Poultry Keeping in India."	...	14
Tyacke. "Sportsman's Manual," &c. ,, 3-8	...	17
Webb. "Indian Medical Service"	5/6	39
Wheeler. "Tales from Indian History."	3/6	39
Wilkins. "Hindu Mythology."	10/6	13